# Ghosts Demons UFO'S and Dead Men
*N. G.*

"19 And when they shall say unto you, Seek unto them that have familiar spirits, and unto wizards that peep, and that mutter: should not a people seek unto their God? for the living to the dead?" Isaiah 8:19

## By: Philip Mitanidis

Copyright © 2009 by Philip Mitanidis
All Rights Reserved

All rights reserved. No part of this publication may be reproduced or transmitted in any form or by any means, electronically, or mechanically, including photocopy, recording, or by any information storage and retrieving system without written permission from the publisher.

For further information or request for permission to make copies of any part of the work should be in a written form and mailed to the following address:

BEEHIVE PUBLISHING HOUSE INC.
2800 KEELE STREET
P.O. BOX 415
DOWNSVIEW ONTARIO
CANADA M3M 3A8

http://www.beehivepublishinghouse.com

Ghosts Demons UFO'S and Dead Men
First Edition 2009
Printed in USA.

ISBN 978-0-9733258-7-4

Published work by the author:

The Creator of Genesis 1:1- Who is He?

The Covenant-A Contract Rejected

No God and Saviour Beside Me

According to a Promise

Christians Headed Into the Time of Trouble

Ghosts Demons UFO'S and Dead Men

Dedicated to: *Jason*

## ACKNOWLEDGMENT & ABBREVIATIONS

All Scripture is quoted from the old King James Version (KJV) Bible, unless otherwise stated.

I have placed in brackets "[ ]" words or a word to clarify the meaning of the preceding word in some references, which I have quoted from the King James Version (KJV) Bible. I also translated the Hebrew word "יהוה" and the Greek word "Κυριος" to read "LORD" whenever the Scriptures refer to God the Creator of Genesis 1:1.

In addition, I capitalized the first letter of the pronouns, which refer to God the Creator of Genesis 1:1.

Greek Scriptures are taken from: Η Αγια Γραφη, Βιβλικη Εταιρεια, Αθηναι, 1961.

Scripture taken from the HOLY BIBLE, NEW INTERNATIONAL VERSION (NIV). Copyright 1973, 1978, 1984 by International Bible Society. Used by permission of Zondervan. All rights reserved.

Please refer to the Hebrew and to the Greek inspired Scriptures in order to verify my opinions.

Front cover produced by Jason Mitanidis

Artwork in this book is produced by the Author Philip Mitanidis.

# PREFACE

Way before Eve broke the Covenant (The Ten Commandments, Exodus 20:2-17), in the Garden of Eden, the archangel (Isaiah 14:12), whose name is Lucifer, better known today by the name of Devil, Serpent, Dragon, and Satan (Revelation 12:9), promised his followers eternal glory, eternal life, and rulers as gods over Christ's created beings who live throughout the universe. But in order to fulfill that promise, first, they had to overthrow (Isaiah 14:13, 14) Christ the LORD of hosts from His lofty throne; (Isaiah 6:1-5; John 12:41) and make Him subservient.

Although Satan failed to overthrow Christ from His lofty throne, and convert all individuals in the universe to his cause, in his frustration, he had to settle for the allegiance of one third of the heavenly angels, and, from the entire universe, only Adam and Eve from planet earth.

After their fall, Adam and Eve realized that Satan's promises of eternal life and the appointment as gods was not true because they were dying! Realizing that they were dying because of their sins, they chose to be saved from their eternal death by accepting the plan of salvation, which was offered to them by Christ the LORD of hosts. But, unfortunately, many of Adam's descendents refused, and still refuse today the plan of salvation because many of them still believe Satan's lie when he said, "4 Ye shall not surely die" (Genesis 3:4).

Thus because of Satan's lie, the immortal soul doctrine was born; and today, as then, the majority of the people throughout the world still believe in disembodied immortal souls.

It is believed that there are many paths to a state of bliss and contentment, to heaven and hell, and the way a soul reaches its ultimate eternal goal of bliss. And the way the ultimate eternal goal is reached by a soul is described by the endless expressions of Hinduism, Buddhism, Taoism, Shintoism, Confucianism, and so on.

Although it is commonly believed by the western cultures that the immortal soul beliefs are predominantly imbedded into the eastern cultures—it is not the case. You will find that the same immortal soul beliefs are also imbedded in the Jewish, Muslim, and Christian religious doctrines.

And, if that is not bad enough, many Christians and none Christians believe in unidentified flying objects (UFO'S). In fact, some believe that these UFO'S are God sent! But, if man has an immortal soul, what is the purpose of a mechanical device called "UFO"?

However, since the majority of the world believers lean towards a supreme being (God), immortal soul, hell, purgatory, paradise, and UFO'S, this book provides true stories* as a prerequisite to the introduction of the soul, ghosts, apparitions, spirit, spiritualism, demons, UFO'S, dead men, heaven, and hell, in order to confront the question of the state of the dead, by the use of the inspired Scriptures (Bible).

Therefore, Scripturally, you will eventually make a decision regarding the Gospel of Jesus Christ and what it says about death and spirits; and when you do, you will choose as to whom you are going to believe? You would believe Christ the LORD of hosts when he said to Adam and Eve,

> "17 But of the tree of knowledge of good and evil, thou [you] shall not eat of it: for in the day that thou [you] eatest thereof thou [you] shalt [will] surely die" (Genesis 2:17).

Or, you are going to believe Satan when he said to Eve,

> "4 Ye [all of you] shall not surely die:" (Genesis 3:4)?

So! Who is lying; Christ the LORD of hosts or Satan?

As you can see from the above verses, one of them is lying to you.

Nonetheless, whomever you decide to believe, you will find this book informative and to the point on the subject matter of Ghosts, Demons, UFO'S, and Dead Men.

The author

---

\*   The stories presented in this book are written as close as possible to the actual events.

# CONTENTS

| | |
|---|---|
| 5. | Preface |
| 7. | Contents |

<u>Real Stories</u>
| | |
|---|---|
| 9. | The Floating Tray |
| 26. | St. George and the Dragons |
| 38. | Would You Adopt Me |
| 55. | UFO'S |
| 63. | Disturbing the Dead |

77. <u>Real or Tricks of the Paranormal</u>
- a). Are Ghosts Real......................77
- b). Are Familiar Spirits Real.............86
- c). Are People Demon Possessed......93
- d). Are UFO'S Real...................100
- e). Dead Men are They Really Dead...111

170. <u>Considering few Objections</u>
Absent from the body........................170
The Transfiguration............................183
Lazarus and the Rich Man....................185
Saul and the Witch of Endor................204
What is the Spirit of Man...................221

227. <u>Appendix</u>
The Use of the Words Soul & Spirit

| | |
|---|---|
| 228. | Questions |
| 229. | Bibliography |

"19 In the sweat of thy [your] face shalt thou [you] eat bread, till thou [you] return unto the ground; for out of it wast [were] thou [you] taken: for dust thou [you] art, and unto dust shalt thou [you] return" (Genesis 3:19).

## *The Floating Tray*

A rifle shot was heard coming from four o'clock; and the echo lingered throughout my neighborhood in the midst of a still summer afternoon. My mother quickly looked out the window from our two-story house; but she could not see too much because of the dense foliage of the trees. She tried looking through one window after another, but it seemed obvious that she could not see the activities taking place on the other side of the street. She tried to peek through the gentle movements of the branches again and again, but could not see clearly the activities to the right of the bridge, or the road, which was on the other side of the river.

Since my mother appeared anxious to see what happened and was convinced that the shot was close to our house and came from the other side of the river, she stared out the window for a long while, and then, she took off without saying a word!

We assumed that she was going to investigate the incident; so we ran to the windows and watched her cross the bridge, she stopped for a moment, looked up and down the street, and then, she ran southward, disappearing in the obscurity of the trees.

My mother was gone for quite a while. In fact, since we were not allowed to leave the house, once in a while, we would get up and very cautiously look outside through the windows to see if my mother was coming home to tell us what happened. But, needless to say, after a while, we began to worry about her because she was gone well into the late afternoon.

When she finally came home, she looked severely shaken, bewildered, and pale. She did not look too good! But regardless of her stressful and pale demeanor, we wanted to know what happened to her? So we asked her in a concerned way to tell us what was wrong with her? And what could we do to help her? But, for a while, she would not be bothered by us. And when she did, after she finally settled down, we asked her about the shot we heard a number of hours ago. "Did she see anything?" "Was anybody shot? And if somebody was shot, who was it?" "Did you see the person?" "Was he dead?" And so on went the questions.

My mom finally said, "What is this some kind of interrogation? I will tell you; just give me few moments, OK?"

We realized that she was stressed out, so we backed off from asking her questions and gave her some breathing room.

After a while, my mother began to speak slowly and nervously. We were told that our neighbor's son was cleaning the rifle and somehow he shot himself and died right there, on the spot, outside of his house. And in a very puzzled and soft voice, she said, "I have never seen anything like it! I have never seen anyone die like that before?" My mom had seen many people die gruesome deaths during the war and after the war. So! For her to say that he died a strange death, it had to be out of the ordinary.

Nonetheless, my mother continued to tell us how the parents of the dead boy and friends tried to stop the bleeding from the wound. But, as they were applying pressure to the wound, they noticed that the blood, which was on their hands, on the boy's shirt, and on the ground, it slowly began to crawl away from their hands, clothing, from the ground, and gently disappear under the boy's body as he lay there on his back on the cold ground. She said, "There was no blood in sight to be seen—anywhere!"

When they saw what was taking place, many, in bewilderment and in shock stared at the boy and wondered where did the blood go? In fear, mixed emotions, and eerie filling, the goose bumps started to surface on many of the observer's bodies. As scared and superstitious many were, they still stood by the parents who were crying over their son's dead body and wondered what was going to happen next?

On the other hand, some thought that the blood entered into the boy's body, and felt, as others assumed that he was healed! But the lifeless body would not move. So! Where did the blood go, many began to question? In fact, the mother of the dead son began to talk to him, as if he was healed and alive! She picked up his head gently from the ground and then she yelled at him; "Talk to me!" But the lifeless form would not respond to her. The more she tried to interact with him, the more hope disappeared from her that her son was alive. And the more she tried to make her son respond to her, the more frantic and sorrowful she became.

Seeing her desperation, some said to her "Let the boy catch his breath." "Don't rush him." "Give him some time," went on the encouraging words of the hopefuls. But it became more evident, as time went by, that their hopes faded. And as their hopes faded, the tears of those who were near the parents began to dry up. Eventually, many began to accept the fact that her son was not going to wake up any time soon and gradually accepted his death.

As the mother backed off and laid her son's head upon the ground, reality was setting in that her son was not healed; he was really dead. They checked to see if there was a pulse, but none was found. The mother even put her head close to her son's heart and listened in her grief for a heartbeat; to her dismay, none was heard.

Sadly because the blood was nowhere to be seen and the wound was healed, people still clung to their hope that he was going to be OK. But that hope continued to dwindle, as the afternoon went by, and even more so, when the coroner validated her son's death. And even after she was told that her son was dead, she could not accept the verdict because she kept saying, "But the blood! But the blood!"

And while she kept uttering the words "But the blood! The blood!" her husband tried to console her as much as possible by saying to her that the authorities do not know what happened to the blood?

To alleviate her concern, they picked up her son's body from the ground, dug around the area where her son was laying, and found no traces of his blood anywhere? There was no blood on his body, and not even on the T-shirt that was used to put pressure upon his wound!

In bewilderment, the authorities decided to take the body for an autopsy to find out if he was rally shot as they were told? Why was there no wound anywhere on his body, especially in the area where they claimed the wound was healed? Why was there no blood anywhere? And since the authorities did not believe their claims, it was important to the authorities to find out why and how her son died? In fact, they thought that there was a conspiracy at work.

Although it appeared to the authorities that there was no evidence of her son being shot with the rifle, which the father was guarding, how were they going to explain the rifle? Did the father shoot him? If so, where are the wounds and the boy's blood? On the other hand, if their claim was correct, how were they going to explain medically his death? Well, then again, there was one hope in the case that could unravel the boy's death; it was the bullet.

They checked the rifle to see if it was fired, and to their surprise, they noticed that it was recently fired. To confirm that fact, they gave the rifle to forensics; forensics revealed that it was fired! Now, the task at hand was to find out if the bullet really went into the boy's body, as it was described by the parents and by those who witnessed the disappearing blood. And, if he was shot, how did the healing of the wound take place on the boy's body?

But, would the parents authorize an autopsy?

When they were asked, to their surprise, they said that they could perform the autopsy only if their son was dead; and if he was dead, they wanted to know if the bullet was lodged in his body.

They agreed.

The authorities, like the parents, became so anxious to know if there was a bullet into the boy's body, they could not wait to hear from the doctors who performed the autopsy. Impatiently they inquired a number of times for the results, but the results were not ready. Then they made the boy's autopsy a priority; they wanted to know as soon as possible if there was a bullet in the area of the body that was described by the parents and by the eye-witnesses.

Finally, the authorities were told that there is a bullet, which they removed from the boy's chest. It matched the unfired bullets from the rifle and the rifle. But, the coroner could not explain why there was no wound where the bullet penetrated the boy's body? Why was there no blood in that immediate area of the chest? Why was there no scar where the bullet entered? And why were no bones broken or shattered from the impact of the bullet?

"You are not making this up are you?" responded one of the officers. "Yeah, you are pulling our chain, aren't you?" added the other officer. "Now tell us what really happened; there was no bullet; right!"

"Wrong," replied the coroner. "There is a bullet."

"No way! Are you sure you have the right body?"

"I knew you would be just as bewildered as I am,"

said the coroner, "therefore I brought with me the autopsy report to validate my findings." And, as the coroner was speaking, he reached forward and gave them the autopsy report.

"No way!" the police officer said to him.

"By the way," said the coroner, "if you solve this mystery or whatever it is, please fill me in; I would really, really love to know how this young man died without any damage to his organs and to his external body. But more importantly, how did the bullet manage to pierce through his flesh and bones without creating damage?"

Meanwhile, while all of this was going on between the coroner and the officers, my mother and the parents of the dead boy could not believe what they were hearing? And during the officer's disbelief, the mother of the dead boy broke out in agonizing tears again and almost fainted when she heard that her son was dead.

The authorities tried to console her; and eventually gave her painkillers to alleviate her excruciating emotional pain. When she finally calmed down, they took her home.

After a long pause, my mother said, "The poor thing. She is still in shock. She thinks that the blood of her son re-entered her son's body and was healed. She told us that they should not have taken her son away. She actually believes that her son is not dead. I wonder how she is going to deal with her loss, after the painkillers wear off?" my mom exclaimed.

After my mom kind of finished telling us what happened, we all, almost in unison, propagated the first question to her anxiously by saying to her, "What happened to the blood? What happened to the blood?"

My mom's multiple answers came in a very soft voice, as she stared at us, "I don't know? We did not get a definite answer. We just don't know at this point in time. In fact, I don't think they will ever know what happened to the blood?"

We all looked at each other and wondered how could that be? "Blood does not vanish—does it?" "Of course not," came a quick reply from across the room. "Somebody made a mistake," another voice stated. Then my mom said, "No it is not a mistake; too many people witnessed the splattered blood crawling away from the front of the body and entering between his back and the ground!" Then my mother added, "Its too bazaar to think about it, let alone to continue to talk about it."

Obviously, my mother was too tired, so we stopped discussing the subject. She got up and went to lie down; but needless to say that did not stop us from continuing the discussion.

We talked about the terrible accident during the following few days; and could not help talking and wondering over and over again about the vanishing blood? Not only us but also it appeared that the rest of the community was buzzing with questions about the disappearing blood and if he was really shot to death?

After the authorities failed to come up with an answer, to their dilemma, like everybody else, they gave up looking for a rational answer, and released the body to his parents with the autopsy report, which stated that the cause of the boy's death was unknown, even though they

## A Floating Tray

found the bullet in the boy's body.

The parents made the necessary arrangements for their son's burial. After he was buried, a number of relatives and friends came to their home to pay their respects to the family in a social way. As people came, they were welcomed and mingled for a while before they were all seated in various places in the house and in the courtyard.

After a while, my mother and one of the relatives, on the side of the mother's dead son, approached the grieving mother and said to her, "It is getting late; we should start serving the people with the food and refreshments."

"Don't worry my dear the refreshments are on their way; the guests in the court yard are served as we speak and shortly, we will be served here."

My mother and her friend wondered why she did not ask them to help her? They offered to help her a number of times but she refused? They wondered who she picked to help her?

With those thoughts in her mind, my mother's friend ventured to find out who was serving the people in the courtyard. When she looked out of the second floor window, she could not see anyone serving the refreshments and the food? And yet, the people had refreshments in their hands. "Well!" she thought, as she stared into the courtyard, "It looks like they are served! Good, but why is it taking them so long to serve the rest of the people? Perhaps I should go and give them a hand to speed up things because it is getting little bit late;

people should have eaten by now!"

As she was thinking upon the events, she observed the people in the courtyard gradually getting up from their seats and forming into groups. She did not think too much about it at first, but started to wonder what was going on when she observed that the groups began to form into one huge group and having some kind of a dialogue? As she observed the activities of the group, her eye caught the movements of the hands of the group; none of them had their beverages? She looked at the tables and noticed that their beverages were on the tables, but more bizarre, she also noticed that the food was hardly touched!

Thinking that there was something wrong with the food because they were all gathered in a group, she decided to go down into the courtyard and investigate. And as she turned, with her mind's eye to the dialogue of the group in the courtyard, and started to walk away from the window, she found herself in the midst of the room in total silence!

"What on earth is going on here? Why is everybody in complete silence?" She thought. "And why are they not moving? Why! They all look as if they are petrified! No, their eyes are moving! And they appear that they are looking somewhere to my right. I wonder at what?"

She moved forward and to the left slowly and continued to walk in the silent room. At first she could not see anything out of the ordinary, until she realized that there were people who were reaching up from their seats and some who were standing reaching out to pick up

## A Floating Tray

food and drinks from a large tray. And then it hit her; she saw the huge tray with the drinks and food upon it, but she did not see anyone carrying it! She looked again, and to her surprise, she saw no one carrying the tray. The tray was floating on air! And as she looked at the tray, the tray would lower before those who were seated and it would rise for those who were standing up to serve them.

As the floating tray moved up and down, my mother and my mother's friend observed, in that movement, a faint transparent figure of a boy raising and lowering the tray, as it moved from person to person across the room.

"Did you see that?" My mother said to her friend.

Bewilderment, awe, confusion, and fear gripped my mother's friend, as it did my mother and with all of the people in the whole room.

There in an eerie silent room, you could hear the mother of the dead boy gradually getting up from her creaking chair, in an effort to try to calm everybody's fears by telling everybody that they are served by her dead son, rather by her dead son's spirit, in honor of his new life.

"Let me explain," she said passionately. "After we left my son's body with the authorities and went home, I was greeted by a strange human outline shortly after we entered the front door of our house. Not knowing what this strange apparition was, I was horrified. But the ghost said that we should not be afraid. Then the ghost said that he is our son in a spirit form; and told us that he came to tell us that we should not greave for him because, as we could see, he was well and alive. He said to us that he only lost his body that was made from flesh; but now, he is in a spirit form and does not need his body anymore. He said to us that he is feeling fine and therefore we should not greave needlessly. I wanted to believe what the ghost was saying, but because of my fear, I could not accept the ghost as my son or the explanation he was giving me.

"Seeing that I was upset and incoherent, the ghost said to me, 'You get some rest and we will talk again.' And then, he vanished out of sight.

"Later on that night the ghost appeared again and told me that he was glad that I was rested. And again he told me not to be afraid. He said that he just wants to talk. I agreed and we talked for a while about the accident and told me that he was sorry to cause me unnecessary grief. I asked him a number of questions; and his answers, it appeared that they managed to calm me from my fears. At that point, I wanted to believe what the ghost was saying to me, but I was not convinced until I realized that he sounded like my son, talked like my son, remembered things, like my son, and knew of the many things that we did together. After we reminisced for a while, he vanished out of my sight again.

"The following day, my son appeared in his spirit form again, and asked me how I was and what I was doing? I told him that I was preparing with the family, food and drinks, for the guests that would come, after your funeral, to pay their respects. Then he said to me," "Are you really going to receive visitors?"

"I said to him, yes."

"But I am alive; you do not have to do this."

"I told him that it was our custom; I have to receive the people cordially."

Then the ghost said to me, "Instead of people coming and paying their respects, they should be celebrating my new life."

I thought for a moment and said to him, "Who is going to believe me that you are alive? They probably will think that I have become delusional and don't want to accept your death. And even worse, they will probably gossip to no end about me every time they see me. Therefore, I don't think it is a good idea that I should tell them that you are still alive"

"You can still tell them that I am alive, not in the flesh, but in a spirit form."

"Again I insisted that it was not a good idea."

Then he said to me, "I have an idea, when your guests come to pay their respects, let me serve them with the food and drinks; and let them make their own minds whether I am dead or alive."

"I told him that it was a vary bad idea because he would scare the guests out of their wits and even worse some might even end up with heart attacks."

"No they won't," responded my son.

"Yes they will—remember; you almost gave me a heart attack."

"You have a very good point. I tell you what! I will not appear as your son, I will remain invisible and you can explain to your guests what was taking place."

"No! I still think it is a bad idea."

"Please mom, let me celebrate my new life by serving your guests and you—please."

"Finally, I consented, and today you are witnessing my son as a ghost in his spirit form acting as a host in celebration to his new life. So, please don't be afraid, take your drinks and food from my son and celebrate with him his new life."

No sooner the mother finished explaining to her guests the situation, her son partially materialized before the roomful of people. At that point, some of the people from the other parts of the house had already come into the room and witnessed the spirit serving the roomful of people with their food and drinks. And as the spirit in its partial visibility was serving the people, it appeared that they felt more comfortable accepting, not only their rations, but also the spirit serving them in his partial materialized form.

Although the guests appeared more comfortable receiving their food and drinks at that point, they were not selective of the choices they made regarding their food and drinks. Seeing that the guests were still uncomfortable, the mother of the dead son got up from her chair again and went beside the floating tray, asked the spirit to completely materialize. And when the spirit materialized as her son, the mother and her son talked to each of the visitors, as the spirit served them. The mother thanked them for coming, and whished that they enjoy their stay with her son and with the rest of her family.

News got around the house of the events that were taking place in the main upper room of the house. At that point, the atmosphere in the room and throughout the house began to be more relaxed and full of curiosity. People began to talk freely about the strange events, as they mingled with each other because they wanted to get the answers they were seeking; and when they did, some were still in disbelief.

Many of the guests, my mother added, who did not hear the explanation of the dead boy's mother, failed to understand the meaning of the floating tray. And as you know, as gossip goes, by the time some of the people, who did not witness the event, in the main room, they already received mixed explanations. And because some of the feedback did not make sense, many began to ask questions, such as, "Why don't all of the dead people visit their families?" "Why don't the dead people stay with their families?" "Why don't they stay materialized so that we can observe them all the time?" "How do they survive?" "Where do they go?" "Where do they stay?" "What do they eat and drink?" and so on went the questions. Everywhere a person went in the compound of the house, it could be observed that the whole house was buzzing with question. Eventually, the question began to spill outside of the house and into the streets.

Needless to say, it did not take too long for the whole community to start talking about the events that took place in the household of the dead boy.

Although the coroner's report did not explain how the bullet was lodged in the boy's chest without leaving a trace of penetration on his body and the cause of his death, it was just as frustrating for many that there was no

*Ghosts Demons UFO'S and Dead Men*  By: Philip Mitanidis
**A Floating Tray**

concrete explanation of the events, which took place in the dead boy's house. But then again, when people talk about ghosts and disembodied spirits, it appears that there is no end of explanations as to who they are or where they come from.

## A Floating Tray

People, it appears, are intrigued with the unexplained, such as ghosts, spirits, and apparitions, irrespective in what form they are presented to them. And yet, only few take the time to really find out who they are? Especially when a ghost or a spirit appears before a person, and the ghost claims to be that person's dead dog, horse, sister, brother, mother, father, grand-father, and so on. Many accept them as such!

Like the dead boy's mother, many people throughout the world, in their ignorance, simply accept what the ghosts (spirits) say to them. And like the dead boy's mother, many people readily accept them, in sympathy, as disembodied spirits of their dead loved ones or somebody else's loved ones.

Having said that, how are you going to convince my mother, and people like my mother, who witnessed the activities of the ghost in the upper room that it was not the dead boy's disembodied spirit?

## *St. George and the Dragons*

I do not know if you are aware of the fact that in many small third world villages, the whole village acts as one local community, just as some of the local communities in larger towns act in unison; people know each other, as if they were part of one big family.

The setting of the following events fall under such a community where everybody knew everybody and acted as if they were all related to each other. And because of that seemingly relationship, most of the people treated each other as friends. And as friends, people asked each other for favors without reservation. Thus the story that you are about to read comes from such a community by a boy who was asked to accommodate a friend on a trip, which he and his mother were taking.

He unfolds the story by saying that we traveled for quite a while on winding roads, and eventually, to my surprise, we ended up visiting one of the churches. We were cordially received by the Greek Orthodox priest, and were asked to go into his office to talk for a while. After that, we were taken on a tour outside of the church. The church was quite large and beautifully erected with all manner of designs on a very large piece of land that had many rolling hills upon it.

After, we were invited to go into the church.

## St. George and the Dragons

Although there were few activities within the church, the priest continued to give us the tour inside of the church. I did not know why we had to know where the washrooms were and where the kitchen was and few other things, but what got me curious was the part when the priest took us in front of the so called most holy place of the church and told my friend's mother that we should pray there right before the most holy place of the sanctuary, during the night, until St. George comes. And when he comes, the priest told her to dedicate her son to him, in his presence. She was to ask him to remove the weakness from her son; and to cure her son from being sick all of the time. And when St. George leaves, she should thank him for his blessings; and when we got tired from praying, then we could sleep right about there, preferably in these two areas of the sanctuary.

I thought, who is coming and how are we going to sleep in here—there are no beds!

After that, the priest took us into his office; and then, he told my friend and me to go and play outside for a while, while he and my friend's mother talked.

Eventually, my friend's mother came out from the church; we talked for a while and she told us that we had to eat something before the night rolled in. When it did, we all had to go inside the church, pray for St. George to come, and pray to him to make her son well.

Then I asked her, "Who is S... George?"

She said that it was one of the very powerful angels of God who went out on a horse to slay the big terrible dragon with a big spear and a sword.

"Is he going to come on a horse to slay another dragon?" I asked.

She said, "Sort of?"

And quickly I said, "When is he coming?"

She said, "Tonight."

"Oh! Is that why we have to stay in the church tonight?"

"Yes, but first, we have to go inside the church to pray to St. George to come, and when he comes, we have to ask him to slay the dragons and heal my son from his sickness. Then, we can all go to sleep for a while, and when the morning comes, we can leave this place."

"What kind of sickness does your son have," I asked her.

She said that she did not know?

"This S…S… this angel with a spear, are we going to see him?"

"I don't know my dear, we are going to wait and see?"

"If I fall asleep, would you wake me when he comes?"

She replied, "Of course I will; I will definitely wake you."

"Thanks!"

When she told me that she was going to wake me, all of the sudden I felt mixed emotions. I thought, what if S…S… George was not able to kill the dragons, were they going to eat us?" So I quickly asked her, "What if this George was not able to kill them, what was going to happen to us?"

*Ghosts Demons UFO'S and Dead Men*     By: Philip Mitanidis
**St. George and the Dragons** _____ 29

She assured me that I should not worry because St. George was capable of not only slaying the dragons, but to also protect us from other dragons coming after us.

Oh! I did not like what I heard; but I did not want to ask any more questions about this George angel because I thought, what if large dragons came to fight him, then what?

Anyway, I kept my fear to myself; she must have noticed that I was worried; so she said again to me, "Don't worry; it will be fine, you will see."

I nodded and then she said to me, "When we go inside tonight, if you like, you can pray for my son to get well; OK?"

I said, "Yeah! I guess so."

"Good," she said, "I am sure my son would appreciate your support. Come along, let us go and eat something before the night settles in."

We went to a beautiful spot, just outside the church, under a tree, whose branches spread out like an umbrella, to have supper, and as we were eating there was not much conversation going on. Most of the conversation was choppy and spaced. But, it was nice because there was no noise or commotion, in the surrounding area, where we were eating, near the church, except for the birds chirping and the animals roaming around. But one thing I noticed; it was my friend's mom, she was not eating or drinking anything. I wondered why she did not eat? So I asked her, "Why are you not eating? Is something wrong with the food?"

She chuckled, smiled, and said, "No! There is

nothing wrong with the food; in fact, it looks very appetizing. The reason why I am not eating is because I am fasting."

"What is fasting?"

She explained, "It's something a person gives up doing for a certain time period or until a person's prayer is heard."

"Do you understand what I have said to you?"

"I guess so!" I responded.

"I am glad you do," she said.

"Now we must prepare for tonight because the priest told us that St. George normally comes around twelve o'clock. Do you think you can stay awake until then?"

I said, "Sure! I want to see S… S… Ah! George and the dragons."

Clearing my throat—Khum—I questioned; "What does a dragon look like?"

She smiled and said to me, "It looks like a big lizard with wings on its back."

"Oh! I like lizards! Some are very beautiful. They come out when it rains and some come out when it is hot outside and lie on the hot rocks."

And in quite soft voice she said, "Not these ones my dear, not these ones."

After we finished eating and played for a while with my friend, his mother said, "Come along boys, let's get ready for our visitors!"

Once we got ready, and started to go towards the church, I wondered what she meant that I would not like

## St. George and the Dragons

these dragons? But then again, she said that we would see the dragons. I wonder what they relay look like? Never seen dragons with wings!

Anyway, it was about eight thirty and the sun was getting ready to hide, as it normally does, behind the mountains. I did not want to go inside the church that early; I wanted to play. But, on the other hand, I wanted to see this George fellow with his spear and the beautiful flying dragons. So, I decided to follow my friend and his mother. We went inside the church, talked with the priest for a while, and then, he told us to stay inside the church and not to go outside during the night. We were to make sure all of the church doors were locked and kept them locked throughout the night. After the priest locked all the church doors, he came back to us, bid us good night, and then he left.

After he left, I asked, "Why we were not allowed to go outside during the night; and why do we have to keep the doors locked?"

I was told, the reason why we must stay inside the church and keep the doors locked was for our own safety; we are not to allow the dragons to come inside the church, they must be kept outside at all time.

"But if the dragons are kept outside, how was I going to see them?" I asked.

I was told that I would know when they came.

After that short remark, we started to go towards the most holy place of the sanctuary. And when we arrived, I felt this eerie feeling because the lights were out and only few candles were lit, which failed to give us sufficient light in the area we were in. But thanks to the full moon, and to the adjustment of our eyes, it appeared that we were not bumping into things and over each other. But then again, holding on to one pew after another was a great help in getting to our destination

After few shuffles, we settled down in the area we were told to stay in. I noticed how quiet and still everything was; even the leaves of the trees could not be heard moving. In fact, the only noticeable movements that could be heard were our own. Every time one of us repositioned or moved over, it appeared as if we were very noisy. I wondered why that was? So we tried not to make mush noise; but after a while, sitting in the dark, even our breathing was getting noticeable noisy. And then, my friend's mom said, "We are nearing midnight. I think it is time we started to pray."

We went into prayer for what appeared to be for a long, long time; and praying for a long time was getting me tired. And in my tired state, once in a while I would look up and see the dim columns in the church, the faint pictures on the walls, and once in a while I would look up, way up in the high round ceiling and see what appeared to be more pictures. And as I was looking around, I wondered if I was going to see the angel George with his horse? The church was locked—I thought—how was he going to come into the church with his horse? And how were the dragons going to come into the church? And why would they fight in here? And how many...

Needless to say, every time I fell asleep, I kept falling deeper into sleep; but I fought the sleep in order to

## St. George and the Dragons

avoid missing the George and his horse. But, unfortunately, the sleep won the fight.

I do not know how long I was sleeping; but at one point, I was startled by a whining sound of a horse, and then, the sound of hoofs pounding, and shuffling. I looked around to see where the angel George was, but I could not see him or his horse. Then I started looking for the flying dragons; I could not see them anywhere? I kept looking around the church, but they were nowhere to be seen! I was so disappointed. And no sooner I turned around to ask my friend if he sees the flying dragons and the George, I heard the sound of the horses hoofs again shuffling and pounding; and as I listened, I realize they were coming from the top of the church. I quickly looked up towards the ceiling, and to my surprise, I could not see the George, his horse, or the dragons. I quickly called out where is he? Where is he? I turned to my friend's mother who was near me and said to her, I cannot see him, I cannot see him; but she would not respond to me. I guess she was too busy praying, so I was left alone to keep looking for the George fellow and his horse?

I raised my head towards the ceiling again; and at that point, I do not know whether I saw the George and his horse, or if it was the paintings that were on the ceiling that I was seeing; but this much I do know, there was a lot of racket, going on, on top of that roof. And after a while, the whining of the horse and the snorting and hoof beating and the, whatever else was going on that roof, it abruptly stopped. There was silence again in the still of the night. It was so quite that I could only hear the

## St. George and the Dragons

shuffle and the repositioning of my friend's mom coming out of prayer. And when she did, she was crying. And then, she got up and reached over to her son, grabbed him gently and held him in her arms for a long, long time.

I do not know how long she was holding him, but it sure felt like a long time to me because I was anxious to ask her if she saw the angel George, his horse, and the dragons. I wanted to know what happened to them all. But she was too busy with her son, so I did not interfere.

I left them in each other's arms; and after a while, I curled up on one of the pews, started to think about the events that took place during the night, especially the commotion on the churches' roof and wondered if the George killed the dragons? And, as I was playing the various scenarios in my mind, eventually I dozed off into what appeared to be a short sleep because it felt that no sooner I fell asleep, I was wakened by my friend who said to me, "My mom said we have to get ready for breakfast."

I looked around and noticed that the sun was out and it was a nice bright sunny day, the priest was there, and few other events taking place. I said, "What time is it?"

My friend said, "I don' know; but my mom said that it is late. We have to leave."

I said, "OK! What's for breakfast?"

"Come on, my mom is with the priest; they are talking about what happened last night."

"Yeah! That was weird; wasn't it?"

"Yeah, my mom was scared."

"She was?"

"Didn't you see her? She freaked out when the noises started; she grabbed me and held me for so long and tight, I was gasping for air."

"No! I did not see her, or at least I think I didn't? I was more interesting to see that angel with his horse fighting the dragons. I did not notice what you were doing."

"Well, my mom is quite shook up; at least that is what the priest said to her. Come on, my mom is waiting for us."

We went over to the place where they were standing, the priest asked me if I sleep OK, and told me to come and visit again. I said OK; we said our goodbyes, and went on our way. And, as we were leaving the church, I felt as if I just came out of a combat zone, in a weird way. Maybe because I was still tired from what I thought was lack of sleep.

But, as we were walking away from the church, I stopped in my tracks, turned around, raised my head, and looked directly on the top of the dome of the roof. I did not know what I expected to see, but after I booked and looked, to my disappointment, I could not see this George fellow, his horse, or the dragons. Then, I thought the reason why I cannot see the dragons on the roof was because they had fallen off the roof to the ground on the side of the church. I started to walk towards the side of the church, but my friend's mother called me; and said, "Where are you going?"

I said, "To the side of the church."
She said, "Why?"

## St. George and the Dragons

I said, "I want to see the slain dragons."

She motioned for me to come to her, and as she was motioning for me to come to her, she started to come towards me; and when we met, she stooped down, grabbed me by my shoulders, looked into my eyes, and very gently, in a soft voice, she said, "The dragons are all gone. You will not find them."

I asked her, 'Where did they go?"

She said to me; "St. George took the spoils with him!"

I said, "What spoils?"

"The dragons my dear the dragons. They are the spoils. Come on let us go and have breakfast; OK?"

"Yeah, but…"

"Come along my dear, let's eat; come on."

## *Would You Adopt Me*

One summer weekend, my friend, lets call him John, approached me and introduce me to his friend, whom I had never met before. After he introduced me to his friend, he told me that his friend lived out of town and has come to visit for a while. And since they were going out, he wondered if I would join them?

I thought for a moment and wondered how long John's friend had been staying with him and questioned why he did not phone me to let me know that he was here, and why the urgency that I should go out with them?

After a brief cordial introduction and short discussion, I noticed that there was no personal information revealed about John's friend, which I found strange!

Since John did not tell me why it was so important that I should join them, needless to say, I became little bit suspicious and wrapped in my thoughts looking for a reason as to why John did not let me know that his friend was in town and why now, he wanted me to go with them? You would think that John, out of courtesy, would want to spend time alone with his friend and not include anyone else in his plans?

Another thing that bothered me was, why John's friend had to be so distant during the introduction? Could it be, one of those things, where personality clashes occur between two people, for no apparent reason at all? Or was there something going on, which John failed to inform me of?

I hopped his visit was not by design.

If it was, what was John up to?

Although there was no serious apparent reason for my suspicion, my curiosity heightened with every word and gesture that was made by John and his friend during the introduction. I was looking for clues with the hope that the clues would lead me to understand why the urgency that I should join them for the afternoon? Then again, I thought, perhaps I was reading too much into John's unexplained invitation to join them. On the other hand, my gut, for whatever reason, was telling me that this was not a normal invitation. But because of my uneasy feeling and curious nature, I decided to go with them to see the sights of Toronto.

After a while we arrived on Bloor Street and started to walk eastward. After a short walk, I noticed that John made it a point to remain close to me, while his friend—I assumed—because of the heavy pedestrian traffic, walked behind us or before us; but most of the time he chose to walk ahead of us.

While we were talking for a while about various subjects and walking on Bloor Street, at one point, John made few religious comments; and suddenly, his friend left us and started to walk a good distance ahead of us. I did not find his move unusual because as you probably already know, most people do not want to engage in religious discussions because they are oblivious to the doctrinal subject of the Bible. Therefore people feel uncomfortable discussing religion. And, like most large cities, the traffic on the sidewalks is frantic. And because these sidewalks are busy, sometimes it is very hard for a single person to make his or her way through the crowd, no less for three people or more in a cluster.

Anyway, John's friend appeared content walking ahead of us. But, at one point, as John and I were talking, I noticed John's friend looking diagonally upward and waving his right hand, above his head, at somebody. I did not pay too much attention to what he was doing; but after a while, I started to ask myself, whose attention is he still trying to flag? And, how was he going to get their attention, in a heavy pedestrian sidewalk, by waving his arms at them? And to further confuse the issue, I wondered, why is he making fists once in a while causing the pedestrians to move away from him abruptly? I thought that he should be careful how he was waiving his fists; somebody could take his actions seriously and end up striking him with unexpected blows! And, if that happens, how was his attack going to be explained, if his erratic actions cannot be justified?

I did not come out to get involved in a mess like that, I thought!

After that thought, I became so involved with John's friend and with his erratic actions that I did not hear a word of what John was saying to me! Noticing that I was drifting away from John's conversation, I thought, out of courtesy that I should start listening again to what he was saying to me; but, more importantly, I thought that we should catch up with John's friend so that we could prevent an un-welcomed incident.

After I caught on to John's conversation, I found myself focusing on John's friend again. Only this time, I noticed, he not only had his hands flying about, but at the same time, he was talking to someone! Drifting away from John's conversation again, I tried to see to whom he was talking to? To my surprise, I noticed that there was no one there involved with him except the passers by!

As you can probably assume, by now, I was oblivious to John's conversation because I could not figure out what John's friend was doing and with whom?

Suddenly, John's friend stopped; and with his hands moving above his waist, he was vigorously saying something in an authoritative manner! At that point, I stopped in my tracks and wondered what was going on?

When I stopped, John was still talking to me as he passed by me. Suddenly, he noticed that I was not beside him; so he stopped, turned, looked at me, came back to the spot where I stood, and said to me, "What's wrong?"

I said to him, "Have you observed what your friend is doing?"

He said "No!"

I said, "Look!"

He said, "At what?"

I said, "What do you mean 'At what?' Your friend is waving his hands all over the place and talking to thin air?"

"So!" John said hesitantly.

I said, "What do you mean 'So!' people think that

he is talking to them? Does it not bother you?"

He said, "No! He doest this quite frequently."

I said; "He does!"

John said "Yeah!"

I said, "Why? Does he have a disorder?"

"Well, not really."

"What do you mean 'not really'?"

John said that he did not have a disorder.

I was puzzled at his remark, at first; so, I asked him to explain his statement.

He said, "I think we should go somewhere and sit down."

John should not have said that to me because he knew how curious I got about things I do not understand. And no sooner he finished his sentence; I thought to myself, I hope this is not what I think it is.

Nonetheless, I said to him, "I am listening!"

He looked at me for a while, and said, "I think you already know what I am going to say; but there is more to the story than what meets the eye."

Again, I said to him; "I am listening."

He said, "Phil, in all fairness to my friend, I want to explain his circumstance in front of him; and I must tell you, he is in desperate need of our help."

I said; "I would do what I can."

"Good," John responded and said, "follow me."

I did; and as we approached John's friend, John said to him, "Please stop talking to your friends and let us go and sit down in one of the restaurants or coffee shops and talk."

*Ghosts Demons UFO'S and Dead Men*　　By: Philip Mitanidis
**Would You Adopt Me_____43**

"But, I can't leave them now. We are in the middle of something important"—John's friend responded.

John said to him; "It would have to wait." But his friend was adamant; he did not want to break away from his, so-called, spirit friends who were hovering above him and beside him.

John insisted; and in a moment of heated arguments, I was stunned to witness that his spirits would not let him come with us!

After a number of exchanged heated words, John turned around and said to me, "It's you!"

"It's me! What do you mean it's me, I haven't said a single word to your friend or to his evil spirits."

"Please watch what you say; they can hear us."

"I know they can hear us, John; but you should have told me about your friend. And, if you had told me, we would not be here, as spectacles, in the middle of Bloor Street discussing your friend's problem with his evil spirits."

"So! What do you want to do? If you do not want to talk about this, I might as well go home because I will not continue our excursion under these circumstances."

John agreed and insisted that his friend break his conversation with the evil spirits.

At that point, not only the evil spirits were mad at me but also John's friend.

Although John tried to stay neutral between his friend and me, I noticed that the air was quite thick all the way to the coffee shop. Even then, at the table, John's friend started to be restless and annoyed even more because now his evil spirits insisted that he leave us.

Sensing that John's friend was uneasy, I said to John, "You know, this animosity towards me is not going to go away."

John agreed.

Therefore I advised him that he begin telling me about his friend's problem, before his friend decides to do something irrational.

John agreed by saying, "The first thing I want to tell you is that I was a medium before I became a Christian."

No sooner John finished his sentence, I could see him gasping for air. At this point, I thought, this is not good; the evil spirits are attacking John.

He took his eyes off me, put his head down towards the table, paused for a moment, took a deep breath, and in heaviness, slowly started to talk again.

While he was wrestling with his breathing, I thought perhaps he was asking for help from Christ the LORD of hosts. I assumed that because John testified that he was a Christian. Satan and his evil angels do not want to see anyone testifying of Satan's existence and of his evil angels; and Satan and his evil angels do not want to see or hear anyone testifying that he or she have accepted Christ as their LORD God and Savior and abide by the Covenant. In fact, they hate and target people who accept Jesus Christ as their LORD God and Savior and live within the framework of the Covenant (Ten Commandments Exodus 20:2-17).

The prophet of the LORD says,

> "15 he that departeth from evil
> maketh himself a prey;"
> Isaiah 59:15

Nonetheless, as John tried to recompose himself, one could see the evil spirit's effects upon his demeanor and upon his friend's demeanor. But John did not give up. He struggled for a while; and as he persevered to speak, his throat loosened and started to tell me that a number of years ago, out of curiosity, he got involved with a group of spiritualist (people who become possessed with evil spirits, normally called familiar spirits). Spiritualists or mediums, if you like, believe that they communicate with dead disembodied spirits. Nonetheless, eventually, he said that he was encouraged to become a medium (a person who has a familiar spirit (s), and by that spirit or spirits, receives information from them, while he or she is in a trance). Apparently, John was encouraged by what he had observed in the mediums supernatural abilities. He came to believe that his fellow spiritualists could communicate with the dead, foretell the future, receive power, wealth, women, and untold benefits. Therefore he decided to become a medium and one of the members of that group. And while he was a member of the spiritualist cult, he met his friend there.

Apparently, at the beginning of John's indoctrination to the cult's beliefs, he was not bothered by the evil spirits to a large degree; but as he began to act as a medium, the evil spirits became more possessive and dictated lot of his actions. And to make matters worse, whenever he tried not to cooperate with the wishes of the evil spirits, he would experience severe migraines, lapses of memory, and was left many times very weak to a point where he could not go to work or do his chores at home.

In his concern, against the will of his fellow spiritualists, John sought medical help, but his doctors were not able to cure him. He continued in that condition for many years and reached a point where he thought that there was no cure for his condition and therefore started to sink into depression.

To make the story short, at one point, John was confronted with some Biblical facts, which suggested that if a person accepts Jesus Christ as his LORD God and Savior and asks to be cured in the name of Jesus Christ, he would be cured. He apparently started to toy with the idea of going to one of the Christian churches to find out if he could be cured.

As he started to think seriously about approaching a Christian church, his problems began to be compounded mentally and physically worse than before. And when he finally made the effort to go and visit a Christian church, his attacks became so evident that he could not understand why his so called friendly spirits were abusing him? Eventually because of their constant abuse, John tried to break away from them but his efforts were thwarted every time. It became evident that the evil spirits did not want him to find out what they are or who they are or get help from a Christian church.

Eventually John and his friend decided to break away from Spiritualism.

"Perhaps by me telling you this much," John said; "you will understand why my friend is in the condition he is in. He has tried many times before to sever the ties with the evil spirits; but for some reason or another he continues to go back to them? I have been trying to encourage him as much as I can, but because he lives out of town, I cannot be there for him when he needs help.

"And the reason he came to see me was due to the concern he had for himself and the inability to break away from the evil spirits. He was wondering if he was ever going to be able to abandon them? He says that he is desperate. He wants to leave them, but it appears from the last time I spoke with him, he has gotten himself even further under their control."

I said to John, "How do you know this?"

John told me that his friend was in the same position as he was when he tried to leave the evil spirits. He explained what happened to his friend, when he continued to learn about Jesus Christ the LORD and of His saving power, the evil spirits began to increasingly harass him. But because he continued to seek counsel and to learn about Christ the LORD, the evil spirits who had harmed his business, now they started to bring customers to him. In doing so, he was overwhelmed with the workload; and gradually, the evil spirits began to interact with him more frequently and told him to look after his customers. If he failed to do that, he was going to lose their business and his livelihood. Forced to keep up with his customer's needs, he started working long hours seven days a week. The overload of work began to leave him weak and tired. But, fearing of the loss of business, to his detriment, he continued to keep up with the workload and abandoned his desire to seek the saving knowledge of Christ the LORD.

In addition, he failed to go to church, failed to seek help from the elders and the pastor of the church, and most importantly, he failed to seek help from his ally, Jesus Christ the LORD.

Eventually because the excessive work left him a number of times sick and unable to do the work, it prompted him to cut back on his workload and started to go to church; but the evil spirits did not approve of his choice to go to church and learn about Christ's love for the human race and for his deliverance from his evil foes. Therefore, the satanic evil angels (spirits) would not give up without a fight. They continued to harass him and to discourage him from going to church.

While he made the effort to go to a Christian church, his business all of the sudden began to pick up even more than before. Again he found himself working long hours seven days a week. And during that period of time, the evil spirits began to harass him even more than before. Many times at night, as he lay sleeping in his bed, the evil spirits would lift his bed off the floor and drop it a number of times to the floor, in order to draw his attention. Other nights, they flicked the lights on and off to disturb his sleep. They would open and close the windows, drop furniture, open and close drawers, scratch the walls, and so on went their devilish work. They tried to keep him awake, in order to make him tired and aggravated during the day. And even during the daytime, the evils spirits would continue with their harassments in an abrupt and subtle way. The harassments continued in various forms for some time making him feeble and stressed out. He could not function at work too well; therefore he was getting behind his workload. He could not complete his customer's orders on time.

While he struggled to break away from the evil spirits, and sought help, he was unsuccessful in overcoming their conniving influence upon him. Then, John said to me that his friend started to give in to their demands and to their abuses because the migraine headaches and his weakness were overwhelming. He tried to reason with them; instead they kept imposing their will upon him, and upon his emotions, by the use of various tactics.

In fact, one night, as he was sleeping, an evil spirits shook his bed, in order to awake him. When he awoke, he observed a silhouette at the end of his bed. On the second look, raising his head, he noticed a little girl about twelve years old.

He said to her, "Who are you?"

The little girl said, "My name is"—hmm, I forgot her name—anyway, let's call her Lisa. She told John's friend that she became separated from her parents and was wondering if he would adopt her?

Puzzled? John's friend asked her, when did she become separated from her parents?

She said, "In seventeen eighty, while she and a number of people were walking behind a wagon in the forest."

"Where is this forest?"

Lisa said, "In a place called Quebec."

John's friend thought for a moment, and then he said to Lisa; "Since you are dead and your parents are dead, by now, surely you must know where they are?"

But Lisa insisted that she did not know where they were?

Then, the little girl came to the side of his bed and asked him again if he was going to adopt her?

He looked at her for a while and said, "Sure."

The little girl started to jump up and down on the bed, hugged him, and then, suddenly, she disappeared!

He got up out of bed and wondered if this was a dream or some sort of hallucination?

He put on the lights, looked around the rooms, and noticed that there were no visible signs of Lisa with the exception of the bed being moved. But was the jumping upon the bed, and the hugs he got real?

John said, although his friend was not sure what to make of the events, he could not help but to wonder, if that night's events were real; and if they were going to be repeated?

The thought of Lisa reappearing kept surfacing in his mind during the day. And once in a while, he would hope, with mixed fillings that Lisa would not reappear again.

During the following nights, there were no

activities, with the exception of the anticipation of Lisa coming back, which kept him awake most of the night. But, subsequently after a week, Lisa appeared at the side of his bed, gently pushing and pulling his mattress.

When John's friend woke, he saw Lisa standing there, at the side of the bed, beside him. He greeted her, they talked for a while and then, Lisa disappeared from his sight. After that event, it became a common reunion; and eventually, John's friend formed, what he thought, a bond with Lisa. And after a while, he was able to talk to her about anything and everything. In fact, he looked forward to her appearing.

After few months of cordial visits, John's friend became emotionally close to Lisa that at one point he asked if he could take a picture of her.

She asked him why?

And he said that he wanted to carry her picture in his wallet to show his friends of his adopted daughter.

She consented, and he took few pictures of her, talked for a while, got his hug, and then Lisa in her usual coming and going, vanished out of sight."

But, meanwhile, I asked if he still had the pictures of Lisa in his wallet. He told me that he did. Then, I asked him to show me the pictures. John quickly stepped in and said to me, "Do you really want to see them?"

I said, "I did."

Again he said to me, "Are you sure?"

I said to John, "Do not worry; my motives are not like yours and of your friend."

Then John's friend reluctantly pulled out his wallet,

gave me the pictures of Lisa, and allowed me to look at them. I looked at them intently and then, I looked up and said to both of them; "Do you know who Lisa is?"

They hesitated to respond, but at the end John nodded that he knew. And while John acknowledged of the fact that he knew who Lisa was, his friend, with a disappointed stare, did not acknowledge who she was.

At that point, I stared back at John's friend because he did not want to acknowledge who Lisa was. In other words, he did not want to sever his relationship with Lisa. He quickly took the pictures from me, put them in his wallet, and possessively put the wallet in is pocket.

Although I disapproved of his actions to keep the pictures of Lisa, I did understand by his actions that John's friend had grown fond of Lisa for whatever reasons. But, those reasons, I feared, would eventually be his demise if he did not sever his ties with Lisa.

I was asked what I recommended for John's friend and I told him that he not only had to throw away all of Lisa's pictures; but he also had to stop responding to Lisa and to the rest of the evil spirit's activities in his life, especially when he knows who they are. I insisted that he had to sever his interaction with the evil spirits because there was no in between stance.

Although John's friend cut my suggestions short, I told John, if his friend's attitude does not change towards the evil spirits, he was going to have hard time to save his friend from his death because sooner or later, he would reach a point of no return. And at that time, he would grieve God the Holy Spirit, to a point, where God the

Holy Spirit would stop interacting with him; and he would be left alone to cope with the satanic evil spirits.

John's friend became uneasy and restless, so we cut our meeting short.

John called me about three weeks later and told me that it appears his friend does not want to let go of Lisa and that he was at a loss what to do about it. And on top of all that John said to me that he to is being targeted with all sorts of temptations and migraine headaches because he is trying to help him.

Now, I am not going to continue writing about these events because it can easily fill this book; but I am going to tell you that the reason John's friend came to see him was due to the fact that some bazaar and life threatening events started to take place, during his involvement with Lisa.

I gave John a number of Scriptural suggestions that he should follow in order to protect himself and how he was to receive guidance and strength from Christ the LORD of hosts in order to reach his friend.

I kept in touch with John quite frequently. He appeared well under the circumstances; and I continued to ask about his friend's activities. But, even though John's friend knew with whom he was dealing with, he somehow rejected our advice and chose not to leave the deadly path he was following.

A number of years later, John got married and moved out west; and regarding John's friend, I have not seen him or heard from him since the last time he came to see John and me?

## U F O' S
~

People throughout the ages have been gazing in the night sky; and many have gazed into the sky during the daytime looking for the unexplained and trying to explain the unidentified flying objects (UFO'S) they have seen in the sky.

In the past, many individuals who had access to telescopes were able to explain some of the things that were seen in the sky; but it was not until the nineteenth century where the scientists were able to explain some of the mysterious flying objects, which crossed the sky; and this achievement was done by their modern powerful electronic microscopes that are perched throughout the world.

Although the scientists in the past were able to see many of the flying objects, they were not able to identify all of them; and today, they still claim that they are not able to identify many of the shiny disk-like flying objects, which have been seen by people of diverse professions throughout the world.

I do not know if you have seen an unidentified object, but the claim that these flying objects have been seen throughout the world is enormous. People from all walks of life have seen them and described them as real tangible objects moving above the ground, above the trees, above the house tops, above the mountains, above the water, and so on go the testimonies of the observers.

Needless to say, the types of flying objects that have been seen throughout the world vary and corroborate the facts that others have seen the same flying objects in deferent parts of the world.

The description most commonly used hovers—no pun intended—around the configuration of a saucer. People have described the flying disks as being round about twenty to thirty feet in diameter, with almost a flat bottom. Around the circumference of the rim, in some cases, it has been revealed that it was different color; and spewed exhaust of some sort. Others said that the rim was solid like the rest of the flying craft. And on top of the rim, the craft looked like a lid of a pot with its round dome protruding at the center of the lid. Others reported that the flying craft, which they saw was more like a spinning top with the same characteristics as a disk but the bulk of the craft was top heavy. Some reports state that they have seen flying objects in the form of a cigar! They to apparently come in various colors and sizes. And some reports state that the flying crafts that were seen were in the shape of a "v," a "circle," a "T," and so on go the reports.

As for the observers of these flying crafts, who have provided mixed reports about the UFO'S, many have stated that the flying objects were noiseless; others have stated that the flying objects had a whizzing sound. Others stated that they had heard a very high pitch sound. But, what is most intriguing by some reports is the fact that people have said that these flying crafts, from a standing still position, were able to accelerate to unheard of speeds. In some reports, it is stated that the flying crafts were seen to almost vanish into space in a mater of seconds.

And speaking of space we have the same report by the National Aeronautics (NASA).

During the Apollo lunar landing, when the Eagle lifted from the moon to dock with the mother ship, the cameras by the space agency was monitoring the event; and as they were video taping the lift of the moon module (Eagle), they had a visitor and that visitor was a shiny flying disk in view. Quickly NASA tried to film the object but just as quickly they tried to monitor its behavior, it flew away into space just as quickly not to be seen anymore. The astronauts questioned the event, but they, and their questions were quickly suppressed; they were told to concentrate on the mission at hand, which was to bring the crew of the Eagle safely home.

Furthermore, some individuals have claimed that they not only have seen these flying objects, but at the same time, they state that they have been inside these flying objects. Unfortunately, only a handful of these abducties have reported that their onboard experiences have not been traumatized. On the other hand, the majority of the abducties state that the various types of experimentations that were done to them, by the aliens, without any medication to alleviate their pain, have traumatized them. And almost all of these abducties who have been traumatized have stated that they had no accountability for the duration of their abducted time period. But, the few, who have somehow remembered the events of their UFO encounter, state that they have been abducted by the aliens and taken inside the UFO. And when they were taken inside the UFO, they were met with tall naked beings with large heads, large black slanted eyes without pupils in them and with large long skinny hands and fingers. Some people also testified that these aliens were small, bald with large heads and fingers. And some also have reported that these tall aliens were dressed with one-piece gown, hanging like a dress, from the shoulders to their ankles. And they did not wear any shoes on their long skinny feet!

Although the description of the size and shape of these aliens varied to some degree, one predominant factor remains in all of the reports, which I have seen, is the fact that almost all of these people who have been abducted, stated that the aliens who had experimented upon them, did not speak; they somehow communicated with each other mentally and by gesture.

Even though some of the abducted remembered the painful experiments that were done upon them, another predominant fact about some of the abducted is the partial loss of memory of the time period they were abducted. They seem to remember parts of the time they were abducted but not all of the time period they were abducted.

In addition, there have been reports that the UFO'S have created crop designs in the various parts of the world.

Although the scientists and UFO chasers have not come up with a rational explanation as to why these crop

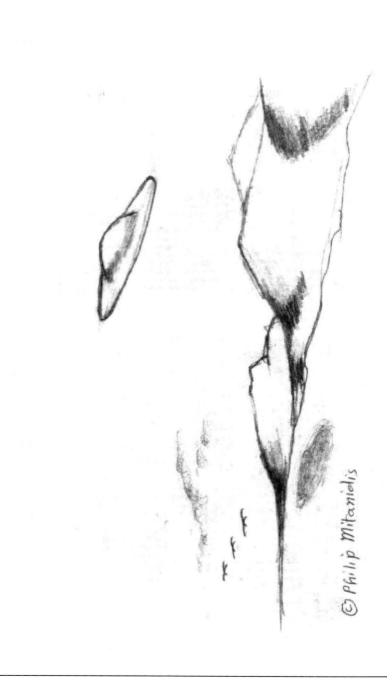

designs were created, they almost all agree that there was no scorching of the crops or mutilations of the crops or any form of chemical compound left behind to indicate that it was the chemicals, which caused the formation of these crop designs.

The obvious question that these UFO'S raise is the fact that these UFO crop designers have not abducted one single individual. Even though I have reviewed over a dozen cases, I am not aware of one single case where there has been one single report of abduction during these crop formations.

Why?

On the other hand, maybe there have been reports of abductions during the crop formations? The Government has a very nasty habit of deleting information from their reports by heavy black markers.

Recently, in August of 2007, north of the town of Estevan, in Saskatchewan Canada, there were over a dozen huge crop designs, believed to be created by the UFO'S, in the various wheat fields.

I wonder how the Government of Canada is going to handle the reports of these findings, what degree of secrecy is going to be given to these UFO crop designers, the meaning of these diverse crop designs, and to what conclusions the government is going to come to regarding the purpose and the meaning of these crop designs.

However the government and the UFO chasers are going to respond to these crop designs, it will be more than likely in two ways; one, the little town of Estevan in Saskatchewan Canada is going to be placed on the tourist map; and two, the paranormal writers will have a field's day explaining their assumptions in their books.

In any case, it has also been reported that these very same types of UFO'S, which have been seen throughout the world, by various people, have also been seen in the fields of the mutilated animals.

The mutilations, if we can call them that are of highly skilled surgical operations. In fact, the mutilation goes beyond the skills of a surgical operation, as it is known by the populous because the removed organs from the animals is so clean that only a laser like instrument or some kind of more sophisticated electronic instrument could remove the inner organs of these animals with such precision.

The selective organs from the various animals, which have been removed, are the digestive tracks, sexual organs, sensory organs, eyes, etc.

And when these mutilated animals were found, after three days or more, it was observed that the animals were not devoured by scavengers or by any of their predators! Why would any carnivorous animal or animals that are hungry not eat part or all of these mutilated animals is a big mystery?

Moreover, the search for answers to these mutilations and why the UFO'S would get involved into covert operations to mutilate these various types of animals have left the authorities baffled. They have not been able to find any clues on the mutilation sites. The authorities have not recovered any footprints, cigarette buts, scalpel knifes, chemicals, or tools of any kind!

All in all, although the authorities deny the UFO sightings, it appears that they have been stumped regarding the activities of the UFO'S, at least that is their report. Whether or not there is any validity to their stance is a good question? But one thing is for sure; they cannot deny the mutilations of the various animals and the crop designs that keep popping up throughout the world.

Strange, if I can use that word, if you were to sum up all of the UFO'S that have been seen throughout the world, you will find them, perhaps like me, intriguing, as to why is there hardly any UFO reports from Russia, India, or China?

## *Disturbing the Dead*

I will tell you a little story as near as I can remember it. It deals with the bazaar death of a boy, in a graveyard, who was in his early twenties.

As you well know, it appears that there are always some individuals in a group who think that they are more superior to the rest of the people in the group. Individuals who think in these terms, about themselves, make it a point to impose themselves upon the rest of the group by bullying or intimidating their way above the group by words or by acts. Sometimes they even go, as far as to take the initiative to prove that they are superior to the rest of the group by doing something out of the ordinary.

On the other hand, a person can also readily observe how some older kids, although they tease and pick at will upon the smaller kids, many times the smaller or weaker kids, in their defense, would dare the older kids to prove to them that they are as fearless or capable of doing some of the things they keep bragging about. And not to lose face, once in a while, the big kids would venture to prove to the little kids that they were not lying to them, in order to draw their confidence in them and sustain their superiority over them. And that is where my story begins, to the best of my recollection.

It was late one night, in a place where a group of kids normally gathered to talk and horse-around. But, on this particular night, the play activities were cut short, due to the unexpected fog that started to roll into the area. Eventually, some of the kids went home. But most of us stayed and gradually found ourselves moving closer and closer into, what appeared to be, a huddle. And as we talked, it was observed that the visibility was gradually disappearing before us. It got so bad that at one point we were not able to see across the street. The dense fog and poor visibility began to concern some of the kids in the group; others downplayed its effects and made fun of those kids that were worried about finding their way home. But for others, it opened the floodgates to tell disturbing and horrifying chilling stories.

But then again, why should this night be any deferent than any other scary night?

Needless to say, one of the boys took advantage of the scary and uncomfortable circumstance we were in and started to scare the rest of us by saying that it was not advisable for us to go home alone, on a night like this because its being said that the dead people (zombies) are going to come out tonight, out of their dusty graves, to take vengeance upon the living; but more predominantly upon those individuals who had abused them and have done them wrong.

At that point, some of the boys who had heard about these horrifying stories became very concerned and asked, "So! How do we go home without being caught by these monsters?"

"It's simple!" said one of the older boys. "We can gather as a group and go to each person's house and drop

*Ghosts Demons UFO'S and Dead Men*     By: Philip Mitanidis
**Disturbing the Dead**

off each person to their home, in order to make sure that nothing happens to them. And near the and, the second last person to be dropped off to their home should be the closest house to the individual who will remain all alone to go home. And that person is me!"

"That is smart thinking," said one of the boys, "but why should you be the one to walk home last? Do you think that you are the only brave person here?"

The boy answered, "That is not the point!"

"So! What is the point?"

"Well stop and thing for a moment and you will see that the closest house, by way of elimination, to my house is Pet's house. Therefore mathematically I should be the last person to go home."

Then some of the other older boys, not to lose face, began to challenge the boy; they to wanted to be the last persons to go home, regardless of the distance they had to travel from the second last house.

The desire to go home last became heated and irritable discussion, amongst the handful of boys; but as the arguments became serious, one of the boys spoke very loudly, in order to break through the vocal debate, and said that they did not have to fight anymore as to who was going to be the last person to go home and be the hero of the pack. Lets settle this like grown men and see who is seriously willing to take the challenge and does not want to lose face, let's pull straws to see who is going to be the last person to go home?

Couple of the boys volunteered to pull straws to see who was going to be the last person to go home. But as they were trying to convince the rest of us that they were not afraid to go home alone, as I stated earlier, there is always in a group one person who deems himself to be superior to the rest of the persons in the group; and this group was no exception. And in order to prove that he was superior to the rest of us, this particular boy, well, he more or less demanded that they did not have to draw straws; he would take the small boys home first and eventually go home alone. But because there were others in the group who wanted to prove that they were just as fearless as he was, one of the other boys went one step further and said that we can all go home without worrying about the zombies; he would go to the graveyard and stop the zombies from coming out of their graves. The group was stunned to hear his bold words.

"What! Are you insane?" shouted one of the boys. "Are you mad?" followed another. "Are you crazy?" said one of the smaller boys. "Are you suicidal?" another shrieked, and so on went the concerned exclamations vibrating through the dense thick fog, which hung all around us.

Piercing through the shouts of commotion, we heard, "I can do this! You do not have to worry about me!" said a proud and arrogant voice.

"No!" "No!" went on the objections.

But the boy insisted that he was going to be all right; they did not have to worry about him. In fact, he replied, "I will see you tomorrow right here on this very spot; so don't be concerned about my well being; I well be fine."

But the group, at least the majority of the boys, would not hear of it; his proposal was way too dangerous. But because few of the boys thought he was pulling a scam; they wanted him to go; and that brought dissention amongst the group; and therefore, during the final argument, they all consented to his proposal.

After the group consented for him to go to the graveyard to stop the zombies from coming out of their graves, those who did not like the boy's outrageous proposal to go and stop the zombies, and for whatever other reasons, they said to him, "How are we going to know whether you went to the graveyard or not? You could easily go home and tomorrow you can come here to meet us and tell us that you went there?"

The boy said, "One way you are going to know that I went to the graveyard is by observing that there were no zombies in town attacking their victims."

"Oh yeah right!" replied one of the boys. "What that probably means is that they will not come out this night."

"Or it will mean that I really stopped them," replied the boy. Nonetheless, "You will have to wait and see; won't you?"

"Yeah right! If you don't go tonight, and we took a chance going home by ourselves, we could very easily be caught by zombies and be killed."

"But, I said that I am going to go! I am not lying to you. Can you imagine how horrible I would feel if I don't go and something happened to any of you? I would not be able to face any of you ever again."

"Words, words," said one of the boys timidly.

For fear of loosing his superiority over the group, the boy thought for a moment or two and then said, "I will tell you how you are going to know that I had gone to the graveyard; go and cut a thick branch from a tree, about a foot long, and make one end into a sharp peg. After you do that write my name upon it, let everybody look at it, and give it to me. I will take the peg with me, and when I arrive at the graveyard, I will hammer it with a rock in one of the graves. And when we meet here tomorrow, in the early morning, we will all go down to the graveyard and look for the peg, with my name upon it, to prove that I was there."

Seeing that some of the boys agreed and others were still skeptical, the boy said, "To confirm the fact that I was at the graveyard during this night and not during sunrise, let us all meet hear one hour before sunrise takes place? What do you think?"

"Yeah, I guess so," some of the boys agreed quietly. But one of the little boys, in the quite moment, out of nowhere, said, "I don't want you to go."

The boy who was going to go to the graveyard was so moved by the little boy's remark that he came forward took the boy in his arms, gave him a long tender hug, and said to him, "I will be OK; promise me you will not worry."

The little boy nodded his head; and after another gentle hug, Al put him down and told him to go home with the rest of the boys and not to worry about him. "I will take care of everything," he said to the little boy.

At this point, most agreed that it was all right for the boy to go to the graveyard, but some voiced their concerns vocally; they did not want him to go. They preferred plan "A," which gave them security as thy walked home as a group.

The dare was overwhelming. I guess it left the boy no choice but to go ahead with his bold act. He said to us, "Its time that you all went home as per plan "A." I will defeat the zombies and after I defeat them, I will look for a descent rock to hammer the peg into one of the graves. After I do that, I will go home and in the morning, I will see you one hour before sunrise right here."

"Do we agree?"

Some nodded, some spoke their mind, and others agreed to meet again early in the morning.

Many of the boys said their good bys and some wished Al good luck; then, very slowly, we all left cautiously to go home, as per plan "A." And as we looked behind us, we could see Al disappearing gently in the fog.

In the morning, before the sun came out, the group, little by little, began to trickle in on the spot where we agreed to meet. And almost every one who came, opened the conversation by asking the question, "Has anyone seen Al?" And the answer was just as anxiously answered, with worried voices "Not yet!" And after the voices faded into silence again and lingered to what appeared to be a silence of eternity, somebody would ask, "Did anyone see or hear anything about the zombies?"

Slowly many of the boys said that they had not heard or seen any zombies.

"Maybe Al stopped them after all." "I wonder where he is?" another responded. "Yeah I wonder?" "I hope he is OK?" "Yeah but why does he have to be so late?" "You know the sun is almost out" another responded. "That is not a good sign" softly a voice stated. "Yeah he worries me to." "Me to." "And me."

"Hay, hay, hay, you guys better give it a rest. Al probably slept in because he was exhausted from fighting the zombies."

"That's right; Nick is right. Come to think of it, we did not hear a single word about the zombies attacking anyone; that means that Al must have stopped them."

"Sure that must be it. He stopped them."

"Look guys, the sun is rising."

"Oh yeah! So it is!"

As the sun continued to rise, slowly the chatter began to diminish into worried-some silence. A person could not only see the weary look upon each person's face, but at the same time, once in a while somebody would break the silence by saying "I hope he is all right?" "I hope so!" another responded. And then, we would go back into silence, as if we all in unison agreed that there is something wrong.

But that was an assumption. We did not know that something had happened to Al. Therefore in an encouraging way, the dialogue centered around on the well being of Al; and once in a while a more concerned voice would say, "I really hope the fool did not go to the graveyard."

The distant dialogue continued to break the silence

and the uneasiness of our discussion went well into the morning with the hope and expectation that Al would finally show up and tell us with his usual rhetoric and exaggeration that everything went well last night. He defeated the zombies and pushed them back into their dusty graves; therefore the town was safe once again from their vengeance.

Unfortunately, our expectation of Al showing up any time soon made us worry even more because people were passing by us, and the time was nearing eight o'clock in the morning.

Because of the late hour, some of the boys thought that something had happened to Al. To alleviate our concern, some of the older boys said that we should not jump into any conclusions because last night was fogy and hard to find one's way home. Besides don't forget, maybe Al got home very late and he is too tired to get up this morning. Give him time to rest; and when he gets up, he will come to see us. Although most of us agreed in a weird way that Al was home sleeping, some of the boys were curious to know if Al did go to the graveyard last night. Then as if there was some kind of silent agreement that we should all go to the graveyard, we all headed that direction. Noticing that we were moving the same direction, one of the boys said, "I guess we are all going to the graveyard to see if we can find Al's peg hammered into one of the graves?"

"Yah, yeah, yeah, keep moving, you are slowing us down," said one of the boys. "Yes you are slowing us down," another responded.

Encouraged by the few snide remarks, it appeared that it took us no time at all to arrive at the graveyard. And when we got near the site, many of us wondered if it was safe to go in. And even worse, some of us thought that Al probably did not come here last night; and maybe that is why he did not meet with us this morning. He is embarrassed. Anyway, one of the boys said, "What are we waiting for? Let's go and see if Al chickened out last night?"

That remark gave everybody mixed feelings; and because of that remark, many of the boys stayed in a group, at first; and then, they gradually began to spread out looking for Al's peg. And, as they were looking, in different parts of the graveyard, there was a great cry of remorse heard bellowing from over the hill, causing everyone to stand still. And then, some of the big boys rushed to see what was happening? Some of us got scared because, all of the sudden, there was total silence over the hill; and to make matters even worse, there was nobody coming back to tell us what was going on?

Seeing that no one was coming back to tell us what was happening, some of us began to look at each other and wondered if we should be going there or not?

After a while, some of the boys crept up the hill to see what happened to everyone; and when they got there and looked over the hill, they stopped moving. Although we were curious as to why they had stopped in their tracks, we were too scared to go up and join them. In fact, they all looked like they were frozen right there where they stood. They looked like they were petrified. We called them, but they were not responding? Cautiously, those of us who were trailing the group began to move up the hill to see why the boys were not moving or saying anything to us. When we got there, we nudged the boys, but they would not speak. Instead they kept their eyes focused in an area located about one o'clock. We asked them what was wrong with them, and in blank facial expressions they grabbed our hands and said to us, "Come on!"

As they pulled us along towards the rest of our friends, who were crying hysterically in a distance, we noticed most of them were near one of the graves. Some were standing; some were on the ground and some were on their knees. We wondered what was going on; and as we got closer to one of the gravesites, we heard the boys crying and saying all kinds of things. We did not understand why they were crying and emotionally perplexed until such time we came very close to the grave and noticed on the other side of the tomb stone, Al was lying on the ground in an unnatural posture. He appeared as if he was trying to run away or something? And then, it hit us; like the other boys, we realized that Al was not moving! Was Al dead, or was he sleeping, we wondered? And then, one of the boys asked the big boys who were there first, "Is Al dead?" He replied sobbingly, "Yes." Then the tears started to come down the little boy's cheeks, who received Al's hug last night; and the rest of us followed. After we cried ourselves out, we all wanted to know how Al died. "Did the zombies kill him?" one little boy asked.

"No!" said one of the older boys, "It was the peg."

"What do you mean?" said one of the boys.

"You see, what happened to Al is something that happens to all of us. We are afraid of the unknown. And because Al was afraid of the unknown, when he came here last night in the fog, he could not see too well. So what he did, as he had promised us, he hammered the peg into the grave for evidence that he was here last night. But since he could not see too well because of the dense fog, as you can see, Al hammered the peg through his coat tails; and when he tried to get up, he felt as if someone grabbed him and was holding him back. He probably thought one of the zombies had him; and in his anxiety and fear, Al died of a heart attack."

"What a waste!"

"No it wasn't," said one of the boys in a sobering manner; "he was probably nailing the peg into the zombies heart."

To pacify the boy's remark, his friend said, "You are right; Al drove the peg into the zombies heart that is why the zombies did not come out from their graves last night."

Calmly, we all gave credit to Al for stopping the zombies' bloodthirsty attacks upon the town's people. After a while, we decided that some of us should go and call the authorities to the scene and tell them what happened.

Following an emotional journey through the graveyard, to what it seemed nowhere, we called the authorities and came back with them to show them Al's body. They asked a lot of questions, took the body, and left us all there, scared, terrified, emotionally scared, and

wondering if the zombies would come out. But, we did not care because we were ready to fight them. In fact, we were so mad, we wished that they would come out where we could see them—cowards!

Eventually, we all dragged ourselves away from the graveyard; and on our way home, we hardly spoke.

No sooner we arrived into town because of the unexplained death of Al, we noticed that roomers already had started to circulate as to how Al died. And, needless to say, some of our mothers who found out that we were involved, they were furious with us, but more importantly, they wondered if we were all right?

Nonetheless, in one theory, to our joy, Al was made a hero. The theory stated how Al fought the zombies that fogy night and pushed them back into their graves by driving the wooden peg into their leader's heart, while the zombie was trying to drag Al into his grave. But the zombie did not succeed in dragging Al into the grave; Al managed not to become one of them by staying above the grave.

Contrary to the coroner's report that Al died of a heart attack, today people who are familiar with the incident, still regard Al's death as a heroic gesture on his part; but then again, some still claim that he should have not died because the zombies whenever they replenish their energy, they will still come out to take vengeance upon those who have done them wrong.

We were warned; be ware of the coming of the zombies on dark summer nights.

# Real or Tricks of the Unexplained
~~~

Thus far, I have provided you with true stories in order to reveal to you that the paranormal exists. And since the paranormal exists, we can ask, "Are ghosts, demons, UFO'S, and dead men real? Or, are they the work of Satan and his evil angels?"

Well, you decide.

For your consideration, I will present factual information for the above subject matter into five parts.

    a). Are Ghosts Real
    b). Are Familiar Spirits Real
    c). Are People Demon Possessed
    d). Are UFO'S Real
    e). Dead Men are They Really Dead

**a). Ghosts**_____ Are ghosts and apparitions real; if so, who or what are they?

According to my mother, and people like her, who have first hand experiences with these types of phenomenon, they will tell you that they are real!

How can I say that?

I can say it because my mother not only has seen the blood of a dead person gradually disappear from his clothes, from the T-shirt that was used to stop the bleeding from the wound, from the people's hands who tried to stop the bleeding, and from the ground. She saw the dead person's wound where the bullet penetrated in his chest. She saw the wound heal. She saw the spirit, or ghost if you like, materializing right before her eyes and served her with drinks and food.

After that event, my mother was pestered by ghosts (spirits) for a long period of time, which I did not know until one night, in another country, where we had rented a cottage for a while, is the place where I found out of her agonizing bazaar ordeal.

What happened that night, at the cottage, was startling for me and very revealing? I heard a heavy weird scream penetrating the wall, which separated the two bedrooms. The heavy restricted scream woke me from my sleep. For a second or two, I was not sure from where the frantic scream came; but I thought of the worst scenarios taking place in my mother's room—a rapist, a killer, a thief, and so on went my thoughts. Then I jumped out of bed and very quickly, in the dark, I opened the door to my mother's room and looked quickly around the room, to only realize that I could not see a single thing!

Then, I thought that was stupid of me!

My eyes had not adjusted to the darkness and I like a fool rushed in the room!

Now what?

I just became a target for the intruder. So! Move out of the way, I rationalized. Move where? I can't see!

As my thoughts were running through my head, at one point, I thought, you know, if there was a killer or a rapist—I wonder how my mom is doing? I automatically looked to my right of my door because I knew her bed was on that side of the room. Eventually, I spotted the outline of the bed. Then, I looked to my left, forward, and then back at my mom's bed. All I could see in the room was my mother laying very still on her back on the bed. Then I thought; there was no one in the room!

Puzzled at the outcome of my search, I wondered if the scream came from outside of the cottage?

Thinking that my mother was still sleeping, I went cautiously outside and looked around the cottage and could not hear or see any movements. Then I thought to myself, maybe I was dreaming and the scream that I heard was in my dream? But, if I was dreaming, why did the scream sound so real?

As I was thinking and walking back into the cottage, another scream, accompanied with struggling groans came from my mother's room. I thought that the killer hid on me in the room, and now, he is finishing the job he started.

With those thoughts in my mind, I flew right into my mother's room, and found myself standing over her. I looked around the room and went around her bed and looked under her bed. And then, I stood beside her and called out to her, "Mom, are you all right? Is anything wrong? Can you hear me?"

There was no answer!

I looked at her and noticed that she was not moving! But the scream came from here, I thought? Why is she not responding—there is no one else here? I reached out and gently touched her arm and called again; "Mom, are you all right?"

After a moment, I felt her arm moving. She

grabbed my hand, and clung to it as hard as she could, and asked, "Is that you Philip?"

I said, "Yes! But, can you tell me if you are OK?"

While squeezing my hand, in a fearful voice and trembling, she said to me, "You are in danger; leave quickly!"

I let go from her clasped hand and very quickly looked around the room; but I could not see anyone there! I called out to her from across the room and said to her, "Where is the intruder?"

She raised her hand and tried to speak but could not. It appeared as if she was chocking!

I ran beside her to see what was happening to her, and when I arrived, she sensed that I was beside her, and in her ordeal she raised her arm again and pointed towards the sealing. Not realizing the significance of her gesture, I looked at the far end of the room, and I could not see anything there but the short dresser.

I said to her what are you pointing at?

She dragged me closer to her face and in her trembling voice said, "They are going to get you if you don't leave!"

"They? Who are they? I can not see anyone in the room!"

She started to heave her chest up and down and with loud grunts and in broken English, again raised her arm and pointed towards the far side of the room; only this time there were movements not on the far side of the room but up on the ceiling. And, as I was stunned to see the activities near the ceiling, I asked, "Who are they?"

And no sooner I asked the question "Who are they?" some started to come towards me. And, as two of the ghosts (spirits) started to come towards me, my mother, as she was gasping for air, was panicking and calling for me to leave the room. But how could I leave her in the room with these monsters I thought. Realizing that these apparitions were the devil's angels (more commonly known as spirits, evil spirits, or ghosts), I right away knelt down and called in the name of Jesus Christ of Nazareth to protect us from these evil spirits. The two evil spirits that came towards me in order to frighten me or do me harm, went back to the far side of the ceiling. Realizing my mother's condition and the reason for it, I asked our heavenly Father in the name of Jesus Christ the LORD to intervene, and to not only disperse the evil spirits from our rooms, but also to stop the evil spirits from tormenting my mother. No sooner I finished praying, there was a screech, a bang, and few other sounds; and when I opened my eyes, I looked at my mother and to the ceiling and noticed that the evil spirits were gone from the room but I did not know if they had left my mother. I got up, went to the wall and turned the lights on in order to see how my mother was.

Looking down at my mother from across the room, she looked calm, but was she all right, I wondered?

From across the room, I shouted; "Mom, are you all right?"

She opened her eyes and nodded that she was all right.

At that point, I was relieved to see her calm; but I

still wondered if her breathing and antagonism was still there? I went near her and said to her speak to me and tell me how you are feeling at this point. She started to speak, but she could not speak freely. I noticed that her mouth was parched, and told her not to speak for a moment. I got up and went to get her a glass of water; she drank it, and thanked me for the water in a mild calm voice. I realized that her speech was all right and asked if she was still having a chocking effect, or if her breathing was obstructed?

She told me that she was fine; but insisted that I was still in danger.

I agreed with her and told her that she did not have to worry because I knew who these ghosts (evil spirits) were; she did not have to be concerned about me because as you can see the LORD helped us. He removed the evil spirits from the room and He has stopped them from attacking you.

Then she asked me, "How do you know who these ghosts (spirits) are?"

I said to her that I have become a Christian and I have learned from the Bible who these evil spirits are and where they come from?

She said, "What do you mean 'You know who these evil spirits are and where they come from'."

I said to her, "Do you really want to know now who they are?"

She said, "Yes."

I was pleased to hear her response; I sat down on her bed beside her, and told her that these evil spirits are angels who lived with Christ the LORD of hosts in heaven. But one day, one of the angels, whose name is Lucifer, and is better known today, as Satan, devil, serpent, and dragon, decided to overthrow Christ the LORD of hosts from His throne, and make Him and the entire universe subservient to him.

But, in order for him to succeed, he had to deceive sympathizers to his cause. So he went throughout the courts of heaven and throughout the universe deceiving whom he could. Unfortunately, he succeeded to deceive one third of the angels in heaven and Adam and Eve from planet earth.

Eventually, once the angels in heaven decided where their loyalties were, Lucifer (Satan) with those angels who sided with him in his rebellion to overthrow Christ the LORD of hosts, they were asked to leave their heavenly dwelling place and go to live with Adam and Eve. They were able to live with Adam and Eve because Adam and Eve gave the dominion of planet earth to Satan for the promise of becoming gods. But Satan and his sympathizers did not want to leave their heavenly homes; they wanted to remain there. On the other hand, Christ the LORD of hosts would not allow them to live there anymore; therefore, Satan (the dragon) and his angels started a war with Christ and His angels and eventually, they were all cast down to planet earth.

The record says:

"9 And the great dragon was cast out, that old serpent, called the Devil, and Satan, which deceiveth the whole world: he was cast out into the earth, and his angels were cast out with him." Revelation 12:9

Did you notice? The prophet of the LORD says that Satan with all of his evil angels was cast down to planet earth. And these evil angels are the ones who masquerade as ghosts, friendly spirits, evil spirits, demons, apparitions of dead men, women, animals, and even impersonate the dead mother of Jesus, prophets, and all sort of dead religious people. And these evil angels, if I may add mother, are the evil spirits that were hurting you tonight."

"By the way mom, why did you not tell me about them before?"

"I meant to tell you lots of times but I was afraid of what they might do to you once they found out I told you."

"You know mom, you have to tell me what else you are not telling me and how you got into this mess; but now you must try to get some sleep—it's almost morning."

Well, needless to say, my mom finally went to sleep and got up shortly before noon; but she needed her sleep and that is why I did not wake her to go to town for breakfast. Anyway, eventually we went not too far from the cottage to have something to eat and then we went to one of the souvenir stores and looked around to see if there was anything interesting.

As we were looking around, at one point, we got

## Ghosts

separated in the store, not too far from each other's isle. Shortly after, I heard a voice saying, "Lady can you talk?" Then I heard a whistle, which depicted the presence of a voluptuous woman. Again, the verbiage followed and said, "Come here." As the whistling and the suggestive remarks continued to come forth, I looked to see from where they were coming, and quickly I went over to the area to see who was speaking. When I arrived in the area, I noticed a large colorful parrot perched on a stand. But at that point the parrot was not saying anything. I looked in the other isle to see if there was anybody there and to my surprise, I saw my mother standing half way in the isle and staring at the shelf.

I went near her and said "Mom," and no sooner I said to her "Mom," she froze; and then she gradually turned around and looked at me with a sigh of relief. I said to her, "What is wrong?"

She said, "I think they are back."

I said, "Who is back?"

"You know, the ghosts from last night!"

I said, "Where do you see them?"

She said that they were invisible, but she could hear them whistle and talk to her.

"They are harassing me again."

Then it dawned on me what was going on in my mother's mind; to put her at ease that she was not tormented by the evil spirits, I told her to come with me. She cautiously followed me and we came to the cage where the parrot was. Then I said to her, "Mom it was the parrot; he was whistling and saying those things to you."

My poor mom, she looked at me, but said nothing.

And then I realized that I was not going to convince her; I started talking to the parrot, but do you know that parrot would not say a single thing in our presence! Needless to say, I could not convince my mother that it was not the evil spirits that haunted her; it was the parrot that whistled and spoke to her.

It took almost twenty years for my mother to accept the fact that evils spirits, ghost, demons, and apparitions are the deceitful work of Satan and his evil angels. But, unfortunately, there are people like John's friend who prefer, at any cost, to believe a lie (2 Thessalonians 2:10-12) because it suits their life style.

**b). Are Familiar Spirits Real?** ___ Earlier I spoke about John and his friend and how they were possessed with familiar spirits (evil satanic spirits); or, devil possessed, if you like. Now, I want to bring to you few examples of these evil spirits from the Bible, which took place about two and three thousand years ago, which reveal who are these "familiar spirits."

Our first story begins about two thousand years ago, in a place called "Paphos," which reveals a certain individual by the name of Berjesus (Elymas), who rejected Christ the LORD of hosts as his LORD God and Savior, and eventually became devil possessed, like my friend John & his friend, like the man of Gadarenes, and like the witch of Endor with what is known as "familiar spirit (s)."

Elymas the sorcerer tried to discourage the deputy from accepting Jesus Christ as his LORD God and

Savior. And because Elymas would not stop interfering with the deputy and Apostle Paul, Paul said to him, "thou [you] child of the devil, thou [you] enemy of all righteousness, wilt thou [you] not cease to pervert the right ways of the LORD?" And because he would not stop interfering, Apostle Paul caused him to be blind, in the name of the LORD.

Here is the account: "4 So they [Paul and Barnabas], being sent forth by the Holy Ghost, departed unto Seleucia; and from thence they sailed to Cyprus. 5 And when they were at Salamis, they preached the word of God in the synagogues of the Jews: and they had also John to their minister. 6 And when they had gone through the isle unto Paphos, they found a certain sorcerer, a false prophet, a Jew, whose name was Barjesus: 7 Which was with the deputy of the country, Sergius Paulus, a prudent man; who called for Barnabas and Saul, and desired to hear the word of God. 8 But Elymas the sorcerer (for so is his name by interpretation) withstood them, seeking to turn away the deputy from the faith. 9 Then Saul, (who also is called Paul.) filled with the Holy Ghost, set his eyes on him, 10 And said, O full of all subtilty and all mischief, thou [you] child of the devil, thou enemy of all righteousness, wilt thou not cease to pervert the right ways of the LORD? 11 And now, behold, the hand of the LORD is upon thee, and thou shalt be blind, not seeing the sun for a season. And immediately there fell on him a mist and a darkness; and he went about seeking some to lead him by the hand. 12 Then the deputy, when he saw what was done, believed, being astonished at the doctrine of the LORD" (Acts 13:4-12).

Later on in Paul's ministry, Paul and Silas arrived at Philippi and ministered there for a number of days. And during prayer a certain woman who was possessed by a familiar spirit began to follow Paul and Silas wherever they went; and often, she would point to Silas and Paul and tell the people that they are the servants of the "most high God, which shew unto us the way of salvation."

But after many days, Apostle Paul was grieved by the evil spirit, which possessed the woman; he said to the spirit, "I command thee [you] in the name of Jesus Christ to come out of her. And he came out the same hour." And when the evil spirit came out of the woman, her masters who used her sooth-sayings for gain, they were not able to do so anymore because Paul removed the familiar spirit from the woman. Therefore they caught Paul and Silas and took them before the magistrates to condemn them. After the magistrates condemned them, they beat them and finally threw them in jail, and put their feet into "stocks."

But, during the night, there was an earthquake, which caused the "stocks" to break open and away from their feet. And when the keeper assumed that his prisoners escaped, he was going to commit suicide; but when Paul saw him, he told him not to because they were still there.

Fear fell upon the magistrates and upon those who accused Paul and Silas of wrongdoing; eventually, they were told to leave.

Here is the account: "18 And it came to pass, as we

went to prayer, a certain damsel possessed with a spirit of divination met us, which brought her masters much gain by soothsaying: 17 The same followed Paul and us, and cried, saying, These men are the servants of the most high God, which shew unto us the way of salvation. 18 And this did she many days, But Paul, being grieved, turned and said to the spirit, I command thee [you] in the name of Jesus Christ to come out of her. And he came out the same hour" (Acts 16:16-18).

In addition to the above episodes, the following event took place about three thousand years ago, in Palestine better known at that time as Canaan.

Although King Saul was admired by the children of Israel (Jacob) and was chosen by them to be their king, he was not chosen to be the king of Israel by Christ the LORD of hosts. Contrary to the council that was given to them by the pen of Moses, in the Torah, the children of Israel chose to be more like the heathen nations that were surrounding them.

They said adamantly to Samuel, "5 Behold, thou [you] art old, and thy [your] sons walk not in thy ways: now make us a king to judge us like all the nations. 6 But the thing displeased Samuel, when they said, Give us a king to judge us. And Samuel prayed unto the LORD. 7 And the LORD said unto Samuel, Hearken unto the voice of the people in all that they say unto thee: for they have not rejected thee: for they have rejected Me, that I should not reign over them" (1 Samuel 7:5-7).

Although Samuel was displeased with the attitude of the children of Israel, he did as the LORD suggested.

Samuel anointed Saul before the elders of Israel and made him a king.

But Saul was a type of a person who refused to follow orders. And more importantly, King Saul did not adhere to the admonition that was given to him by Christ the LORD of hosts. Most of the time, he did his own thing in order to please his subjects, so that he would find favor in their sight instead of the LORD of hosts. Therefore he disobeyed the word of the LORD on numerous times, which became easier, as time went on.

Eventually, King Saul removed himself spiritually from the LORD. In doing so, the blessings and the protection were removed by the LORD. And when that happened, the Philistines, prompted by satanic influence, went to war with the Israelites. In desperation, King Saul sought the LORD of hosts, but the LORD would not answer him. Fearful and in despair, that he was going to lose the war because he was not getting the support from the LORD, he summoned couple of his generals, which he trusted, and told them to go and seek a person who had a familiar spirit.

In secrecy, they went and found a woman who had a familiar spirit and told King Saul that there is a woman with a familiar spirit, who lives in Endor. (Endor is located north of Jerusalem.)

As soon as King Saul heard the news, he made arrangements to go during the night to see her. He disguised himself, to avoid recognition by the public.

The record of King Saul's actions is revealed in the following verses: "3 Now Samuel was dead, and all Israel

## Are Familiar Spirits Real

had lamented him, and buried him in Ramah, even in his own city. And Saul had put away those that had familiar spirits, and the wizards, out of the land. 4 And the Philistines gathered themselves together, and came and pitched in Shunem: and Saul gathered all Israel together, and they pitched in Gilboa. 5 And when Saul saw the host of the Philistines, he was afraid, and his heart greatly trembled. 6 And when Saul enquired of the LORD, the LORD answered him not, neither by dreams, nor by Urim, nor by prophets.

> "7 Then said Saul unto his servants, Seek me a woman that hath a familiar spirit, that I may go to her, and enquire of her. And his servants said to him, Behold, there is a woman that hath a familiar spirit at Endor.

"8 And Saul disguised himself, and put on other raiment, and he went, and two men with him, and they came to the woman by night: and he said, I pray thee divine unto me by the familiar spirit, and bring me him up, whom I shall name unto thee. 9 And the woman said unto him, Behold, thou [you] knowest what Saul hath done, how he hath cut off those that have familiar spirits, and the wizards, out of the land: wherefore then layest thou a snare for my life, to cause me to die? 10 And Saul sware to her by the LORD, saying, As the LORD liveth, there shall no punishment happen to thee for this thing.

"11 Then said the women, Whom shall I bring up

unto thee? And he said, Bring me up Samuel. 12 And when the woman saw Samuel, she cried with a loud voice: and the woman spake to Saul, saying, Why has thou [you] deceived me? for thou art Saul. 13 And the king said unto her; Be not afraid: for what sawest thou? And the woman said unto Saul, I saw gods ascending out of the earth. 14 And he said unto her, What form is he of? And she said, An old man cometh up; and he is covered with a mantle. And Saul perceived that it was Samuel, and he stooped with his face to the ground, and bowed himself" (1 Samuel 28:3-14).

The satanic familiar spirit who impersonated Samuel (v.8), as you have read, did not give King Saul any advice; he stated the obvious that he was going to kill him on the battlefield (v.19).

Hearing the devastating words of Satan, Saul, in his anxiety, fell to the ground helpless. He had no one to turn to for his deliverance. Tomorrow, he and his two sons will all be dead. The satanic familiar spirit did not offer any mercy. King Saul was not only going to lose his throne, which he guarded so possessively, but he was also going to die.

It did not have to be that way. Saul should not have accepted the throne of Israel, in the first place, if he was not willing to abide by the word of the LORD. Christ the LORD of hosts would not allow the whole nation of Israel to be destroyed by the self-serving inventions of King Saul. Therefore the LORD allowed the Philistines to overcome the army of Israel and removed her rebellious king from the throne.

**Demon Possessed**

Historically and Scripturally, the above Biblical presentations are real. Paul and Barnabas encountered Elymas the sorcerer in a place called "Paphos."

Later Apostle Paul and Silas encountered the woman at Philippi who had a familiar spirit

The war between the Philistines and Israel was real. The death of King Saul and his sons were real. The witch of Endor was also real. But if you do not believe in witches or in evil spirits, consider the following verse: "9 And the great dragon was cast out, that old serpent, called the Devil, and Satan, which deceiveth the whole world: he was cast out into the earth, and his angels were cast out with him" (Revelation 12:9).

The prophet of the LORD warns: "14 And no marvel: for Satan himself is transformed into an angel of light" (2 Corinthians 11:14). Therefore Satan and his evil angels are the ones who impersonate dead people and go around the world to deceive whom they can. "14 For they are the spirits of devils, working miracles, which go forth unto the kings of the earth and of the whole world, to gather them to the battle of that great day of God Almighty" (Revelation 16:14).

**c). Are People Demon Possessed** Are there people who are really demon possessed today?

Few years ago, there was a man in a little town who did unthinkable cruel things to himself and to others. Most people did not know why the man did harm to himself, to a degree of lunacy, and what appeared to be suicidal tendencies, many times over. But roomer had it that this man was possessed with demons, who caused him to act violently and irrationally.

Although during my younger days I did not know what it meant for a person to be demon possessed, now I can give you a parallel scenario, which took place in a town that was located in a place called Gadarenes. This town is on the east side of the Lake of Galilee, about half way down the lake, and north of decapolis (10 cities).

This town, like most towns, had its graveyard placed outside of the town's peripheral limits. And there in the graveyard lived two demon-possessed men, which scared many of the town-folk whenever they had to be in the vicinity. In fact, whenever people were in the vicinity coming from the fields and orchards or going to them, if the two demon possessed men were there, they would not let the town folk pass by.

Because the two demon-possessed men were exceedingly fierce, the town's people were not only scared from these two demon-possessed men but the women were afraid from one of the demon-possessed man in particular because he ran around the tombs and countryside naked trying to draw the passersby their attention. And since the demon-possessed man would not put on clothes, stop harassing the women, stop terrorizing the people to do them harm, the town's people decided to capture him and confine him. And when that did not work, they decided to recapture the man, bind him with ropes, in a restricted manner, so that he would not be a serious threat to anyone. But to their surprise, every time they bound him with ropes, he would break them. Then they tried to confine him with chains; to their surprise that did not work either because he also broke the chains and the fitters in pieces. They tried to contain him with heavier chains and fitters, but they could not; he continued to break them. Finally, in fear, they stopped trying to restrain him.

The awesome power that was instilled in him by the demons, and the ability to break the chains and fitters, terrorized the town's people even more. They were afraid to run into him.

Another reason why most people were afraid of him was due to his horrid appearance, the yelling, the screaming, and the crying in pain, which he caused upon himself by cutting himself, throwing himself upon the jagged rocks, thorns, and whatever other objects he could find to do himself harm. And when people saw him naked, bleeding, tormented in excruciating pain, and screaming for help, most people found the naked demon-possessed man fearfully repulsive and perplexing? Therefore he did not get the help he was seeking from the passers by or from the people of the nearby town.

So! Why did this demon-possessed man harm himself so severely?

Well, stop and think for a moment; if you were tormented mentally and in pain by the demons, which possessed you, day in and day out, and thought that there was no hope of deliverance from your demon possessed ordeal, you probably would reach a point in your life where you would start thinking of ways to commit suicide. Obviously this demon-possessed man reached that point in his tormented life; he finally wanted to end it. But even worse, the demons, which possessed him, would not permit him to succeed. And that drove the man in a mad mental state and into desperation.

Although I do not know what the outcome is of the demon possessed man today, in the village, which I mentioned earlier, and by how many demons he was possessed; but, in this case, the demon-possessed man in Gadarenes was possessed by over two thousand demons! Here is the account: "AND they [the disciples and Jesus Christ the LORD of hosts] came over unto the other side [east side of the lake] of the sea [Lake of Galilee], into the country of the Gadarenes. 2 And when He was come out of the ship, immediately there met Him out of the tombs a man wit.h an unclean spirit, 3 Who had his dwelling among the tombs: and no man could bind him, no, not with chains: 4 Because that he had been often bound with fetters and chains, and the chains had been plucked asunder by him, and the fetters broken in pieces: neither could any man tame him. 5 And always, night and day, he was in the mountains, and in the tombs, crying, and cutting himself with stones. 6 But when he saw Jesus afar off, he ran and worshipped Him. 7 And cried with a loud voice, and said, What have I to do with Thee Jesus, Thou Son of the most high God? I adjure Thee by God, that Thou torment me not. 8 For He said unto him, Come out of the man, thou unclean spirit. 9 And He asked him, What is thy [your] name? And he answered, saying, My name is Legion: for we are many. 10 And he besought Him much that He would not send them away out of the country.

"11 Now there was there nigh unto the mountains a great herd of swine feeding. 12 And all the devils besought Him, saying, Send us into the swine, that we may enter into them. 13 And forthwith Jesus gave them leave. And the unclean spirits went out, and entered into the swine: and the herd ran violently down a steep place into the sea, (they were about two thousand;) and were choked in the sea [lake].

"14 And they that fed the swine fled, and told it in the city, and in the country. And they went out to see what it was that was done, 15 And they come to Jesus, and see him that was possessed with the devil, and had the legion, sitting and clothed, and in his right mind: and they were afraid. 16 And they that saw it told them how it befell to him that was possessed with the devil, and also concerning the swine. 17 And they began to pray Him [Jesus Christ the LORD of hosts] to depart out of their coasts" (Mark 5:1-17).

In the above events of the naked demon-possessed man, we are told that at one point in his life, when he was seeking help, he got it from someone who had "compassion" upon him and was not afraid of him.

We are told when the man heard that Jesus Christ the LORD was coming, he went to meet Jesus; and when he was approaching Jesus, the demons who possessed the tormented man, acknowledged who Christ was and falsely accused Jesus by saying that He was going to torment them before their time. And, as the demons continued to suppress the tormented man because the demon possessed man had heard about Jesus and of the miracles He had performed, he struggled against the demons who continued to suppress his speech and prevailed. And when he did, he asked Jesus to deliver him from the demons who possessed him. In compassion, Jesus called the demons out from the abused naked man; but the demons did not want to leave their dwelling place, which was within the tormented naked man. But the command of Jesus could not be avoided, so they asked Jesus not to send them to another country because if He did, they would most likely not find another person to possess right away, therefore they would suffer in the earth's harsh environment. The earth's ecosystem and atmosphere is too dry for them to be exposed for too long that is why they seek men, women, and some animals to dwell in; but preferably, they desire to inhabit people because they can receive pleasure from them through their sensory organs. At the same time, the demons (evil angels) receive pleasure by causing them to do all sorts of evil acts, in order to draw them away from Christ's saving power, and to cause Christ pain when they succeed to divert the people they possess away from Him and from His eternal salvation.

Knowing that Jesus would not bid them leave into another human being, and did not want to be sent to another country, the demons requested that they be allowed to inter the herd of pigs that were not too far from them. And when they did, all of the swine in the countryside went wild in pain and ran right into the lake and drowned.

## Demon Possessed

When the people saw what happened to the herd, the keepers of the swine went and told their owners what happened. When they did, they all came to Jesus and told Him to leave. They were not interested in the Gospel of Jesus Christ; they preferred to save their pig industry.

But, there was somebody in that town who did appreciate Jesus with thankfulness of heart; and that person was the naked demonic possessed man, who now was dressed and in his right mind. In fact, he wanted to go with Jesus and be His disciple. But, Jesus told him to go and tell the people and his friends of the great things Jesus Christ the LORD had done for him.

Dressed and in his "right mind," calm and collective, the man complied to Jesus' request, and went into the town to tell the people and his friends "what God had done for him."

Although the above narrative reflects upon a demon possessed man who lived about two thousand years ago, are there any demon possessed men and women today?

Unfortunately, the answer is yes!

As you probably already know, there are numerous demon possessed men and women who live throughout the world of ours. They are with us and they will continue to be with us until Satan and his evil angels are consumed by fire and "be no more."

**d). Are UFO'S real**_____ Close above the Brazilian mountains, there were three silvery flying disks, about thirty feet in diameter, captured, in a close up, by the camera and reproduced in a vivid picture.

Although the three flying disks were tangible and real, the news media was skeptical about the three shiny disks, as being the product of human ingenuity. Therefore they were identified as flying saucers, flying disks, and space ships because earthly powers disclaimed them and of their existence. And because of their disclaimer, they were identified as unidentified flying objects (UFO'S) and many placed them in the category of the paranormal.

At that time, even though the populous was curious, as to what these objects were, not much was made ado until nineteen forty-seven when the residents of Roswell, New Mexico, USA, found a crashed disk, which resembled the three flying metallic disks above the Brazilian mountains. The residents of New Mexico, not only found a crashed disk, but they also found, on the site, three four feet tall, so-called, aliens.

People, radio, magazines, and newspapers had a field-day with that finding. But, very quickly, the armed forces moved in, took over the site, and restricted the curious from viewing it. The UFO, with its passengers, was taken away in secrecy; and the site was quickly cleaned up by the armed forces, leaving no traceable presence of the UFO.

Needless to say, the armed forces and the government authorities still deny the crash landing of a flying disk, in Roswell New Mexico, even today. But because the residents of Roswell knew first hand what they saw, the news continued to spread very quickly throughout the area of the flying disk and its passengers.

And those who heard the news for the first time, they made a point to come and see the site, to only find themselves turned away from the area by the government authorities, where the flying disk had crashed. The news spread just as quickly that the armed forces were hiding something from the public because they would not allow visitors to approach the UFO site. The authorities feared that the curious would find something from the flying disk, as evidence of its existence; therefore, they barred visitors from the site for a number of months, but continued to monitor the activities of the ranchers in the area and the visitors to the site.

Although the authorities denied what was found on the site, the people of Roswell began to make postcards of the UFO and of its four-feet high aliens. Eventually, the proprietors of the area began to sell all kinds of paraphernalia depicting the UFO and the three aliens. In fact, even today, if you were to go to Roswell, in New Mexico, you will find all kinds of paraphernalia in their souvenir stores, and an annual event, which brings people from all over the world once a year to dress in their favorite alien costumes.

But, the Roswell UFO phenomenon did not stop with its local hype. In the sixties, the UFO craze mushroomed throughout the world, believing that we are not alone. In fact, it got so bad that there were, and still are today, factions who believe and wait for the coming of the aliens to land any minute on planet earth, in order to stop us from blowing ourselves into oblivion with our own arsenal—so say the enthusiasts.

But, even weirder, if I can use that word, is the continuation of the constant watch of the sky for a sign of their coming. In fact, the UFO phenomenon sprung groups of followers into such an intense following that some of the groups turned their faith into a religious following.

Recently, as you probably know, many have died in California when a comet named "Hail-Bob" was revealed to be heading towards planet earth. One of the groups, in California, thought that the comet was the mother space ship or the comet contained the aliens who have come to briefly monitor the earth's activities and when they finished their work they were to go back to their own world. And when the comet came and was passing over the earth, this group of believes committed suicide. The reason they committed suicide was due to the fact that they were duped to believe that when they killed themselves, they were going to release their spirits from their bodies in order to enable them to go up into the space ship and join the aliens. The reason they wanted to join the aliens was due to their passionate desire to live in a civilized world in some form of utopia.

So! Did these UFO believers hitch a ride in a space ship (UFO)?

Are they living in another world?

Tragically, empirically, and tangibly, obviously not

because the scientific community that was monitoring the comet, found no life forms or a space ship on it or in it. The comet was made from some debris and mostly of solid ice, which left increasingly a huge trail behind it, due to the sun's intensifying heat, as it passed by planet earth.

As for the believers, they all died a needles death.

In another scenario, in a quite sleepy little town, the radar in the air force base began to act up erratically. "This cannot be right!" The radar attendant muttered under his breath. But, as procedures go, he had to report the malfunction to his superiors. The bleep on his radar, now stopped moving? How can it suddenly stop moving in mid air, when it was moving in extreme speed? The radar attendant responded in bewilderment! He could not question the erratic activities on his radar anymore, so he quickly communicated his observation to his commanding officer. His officer quickly questioned if the activities on his radar were abnormal due to malfunction or was there something out there?

"My opinion Sir, there is something moving out there."

In response, his superior said, "Have your equipment checked." And then in the next breath, the officer ordered a red alert. And no sooner the sirens began to scream, off went the pilots in their jets as they were ordered to scramble. The co-ordinates were given to the pilots, as they were taking off to meet the intruder in their air space. Some pilots were ordered to protect the air base. Some went thrusting upwards into the sky, gaining rapped altitude. Once the pilots reached their designated altitude, they leveled off and pursued the co-ordinates in the sky where the intruder had moved into.

    As the jet fighters were heading to their destination, the commanding officer asked the pilots if they had the flying object on their radar? The pilots stated that the object was in their radar and in a mater of seconds they would have visual contact. And when they did, the pilots reported a metallic disk hovering in the sky. But no sooner the pilots reported the flying object on their sight, the UFO dropped downwards out of sight in a matter of seconds. The pilots were stunned to see the UFO move so quickly from standing still to some unheard of speed. One of the pilots exclaimed, "Did you see that!" "Yeah!" said another, as they adjusted their flight path to pursue the UFO; but when they finally dropped to the UFO'S level, to their surprise, they found the UFO was standing still in one spot waiting for them. Again, no sooner the pilots tried to communicate with the UFO, the UFO moved away from them to another spot and stopped in mid air to wait for the jets to arrive.

    The object that was being tracked by the radars at the base and by the pilots, moved at unheard of speeds; and then, as if at will, it stopped on a dime, abruptly, in mid air! The radars on the air base mirrored the same moves on the radar in the cockpit of the jets. The pilots were not seeing things. The UFO was not only moving very rapidly away from the jets, but it appeared that the UFO was toying with the pilots while they pursued it.

    Seeing that the UFO was too agile in its maneuvers, the commanding officer ordered the pilots to encircle the

UFO and fire upon it.

On their commander's command, the pilots scrambled to their new positions and made ready to attack the UFO, which was standing still, and what appeared, waiting for them to come. As the jets moved on the intruder and locked the target on their weapon's screen, their electronic equipment started to act erratic and eventually it malfunctioned. Finally, the target became visible, but they were not able to fire upon it, as if to say, you cannot do anything to me. And, as the jets were moving rapidly upon the UFO, the UFO, as if at will, suddenly moved out of the way, stopped, and then, took off diagonally upwards in blazing speed. And when it did, the UFO shook one of the airplanes violently from its flight path. And when the pilot saw the UFO go by him in enormous speed, he exclaimed, "What was that!" And when the pilot looked at his radar screen (HUD), the instruments and the radar went nuts. Shortly after, with enormous energy and will power, the pilot managed to stabilize his aircraft. He made contact with the other pilots, and found out that they to lost control of their airplanes, but now, they are all right; unfortunately, they lost sight of the UFO. In fact, neither the air base nor the pilots had a clue where the UFO went. Their radars, although normal, at this point, were not detecting the UFO.

The pilots remained in the air and continued to scan the sky with their instruments with the hope that they would eventually find where the UFO went. They stayed in the sky until they were almost out of fuel and then they returned to base. Although their jets were grounded, the air force remained on the alert and continued to scan the sky for the intruder.

There are many visual sightings of flying metallic discs throughout the world, I do not know how you or I can tell someone who has seen these UFO'S or been in them that they are not real or they do not exist?

How would you rationalize the shadow a UFO casts upon the ground or upon the water or upon your house, if the UFO is not real? How do you deny the sound you hear from these flying objects or the various colors they propagate as they hover or fly at extraordinary speed? What do you say to the many pilots who have seen flying disks, during world war two, flying beside their airplanes? What do you say to the astronauts who have seen various types of flying disks? And what do you say to the commercial pilots who have seen these flying disks. What do you say to the Air Force commanders who got the getters on numerous occasions when their radar revealed flying disks in their air space? And what about the Air Force pilots who have seen these flying disks and were ordered to retaliate against them to only find out that they were no match against them?

It has being reported, time after time that these flying saucers moved out of sight in unheard of speeds. They were able to outrun the missiles that were fired upon them and even cause the aircraft, which fired upon them to malfunction. And what about the civilians of the world who have seen these flying objects; do you think they like the astronauts and pilots are delusional? Are the pictures

*Ghosts Demons UFO'S and Dead Men*   By: Philip Mitanidis
**Are UFO'S Real**

that are captured by film, cameras, videos, and digital cameras delusional also? And, if you like, you can call me delusional also because I have seen a UFO.

So! How do you convince me that I have not seen a UFO?

And, if am delusional, how do you explain the gradual disappearance of the UFO behind the cluster of trees, as I followed its flight path so vividly above the nearby trees.

As I watched this huge noiseless disk, gradually, little by little disappearing behind the trees, it glued my eyesight to the tops of the trees for a long, long time. As I wondered where it went, I thought, it should have surfaced by now, unless it landed or crashed?

Needless to say, I continued to look for the appearance of the flying object, but I failed to see it again.

So, are UFO'S real, are aliens real. Or are they the product of man, whose sophistication is kept a secret, like the many advanced military arsenals?

I do not know if you know that United States of America (USA) and Britain have been working together on military projects, more predominantly, ever since world war two was imposed upon the citizens of planet earth. And of late, you can see more readily that the USA and Britain are working hand in hand politically and militarily. In fact, Canada, which is part of the British colonies, and United States of America had a joint venture on building these flying disks (Avrocars) in Canada during the nineteen fifties, in a place called Malton Ontario, now changed to Mississauga Ontario.

After spending over ten million dollars on the flying disk project and a number of failed experiments to make the unstable Avrocar fly successfully, the USA pulled out of the contract in 1961. That move made the unions very mad, and eventually, the Progressive Conservative party was kicked out of office. But in the interim, many individuals, who were laid off, took their High-Tec skills and found work in the USA.

Today, one of the flying disks that was revealed to the news media, before they closed the assembly of the flying disk (Avrocar) and the research facility in Malton Ontario, is placed in Ft. Eustis Transportation museum in Virginia USA. And another flying disk is believed to be currently kept in Garber Restoration museum, Maryland.

Today, military personnel do the assembling of these flying disks in secrecy. The only time these flying disks are seen is when they are used to test their maneuverability and capability in all manner of situations. And since the technology of these flying machines is so far advanced, they have replaced the jet fighters and closed their Top Guns schools. In fact, Britain and America are not going to build any more manned jet fighters because they, in comparison to the flying disks, have become obsolete. The last jet fighters built jointly by Britain and USA are the F-22 and F-32.

Now Britain and America have created flying saucers that vary in size. They range from sixty feet to six inches. But even more radically, they have created at Berkley, engines that are smaller that a shirt button, which can produce enormous, thrust of power for miniature flying disks. In fact these small flying machines are able to reach their targets with uncanny accuracy and speed by the use of a remote control that is held thousands of miles away. And when these flying machines are armed with deadly bombs, they can hit their targets every time with precise accuracy.

These small flying machines can be flown into chimneys, windows, doors, vents, and so on without aborting their target.

But, if these flying machines are man made, how are they able to withstand the extreme gravity pull they create upon those individuals that are in them?

The answer is simple; the scientists have overcome the gravity pull by simply turning a switch on. In doing so, the passengers and pilots are placed in a natural atmosphere; and they do not have to worry about the effects of gravity upon them. Therefore, they are able to travel with their flying machines in extreme speeds.

A lot more can be said about Britain's and America's flying disks and about their electronic high Tec and electronic flying gadgetry; but this much I do know, sooner than later because of the tension and wars across the ocean, these sophisticated flying objects will surface as the arsenal of war of the west and of the east (Russia).

Why did I include Russia?

I included Russia in the UFO equation because as you probably already know, when the Russians over ran the German army, and a remnant was pushed back into Germany, Hitler ordered all of the scientific research and developments destroyed; and that included the flying saucers. Although the order was carried out, what were not destroyed were the scientists that were working on these projects.

When the Russians came to Germany, they recruited many of these scientists and placed them into their Russian scientific laboratories. There, the German and Russian scientists, not only placed a "sputnik" in orbit, in the fifties, but also developed the flying saucers, better known as UFO'S. And when the west learned of the Russian developments, they quickly poured millions of dollars into their laboratories and manpower. And since the west had also recruited some of the German scientists, they were approached to help speed up the space race and develop a flying saucer.

The first effort to develop a flying saucer, by the west, as it was stated before, it was contracted, for political purposes, to a Canadian firm in Ontario; but more covertly, it was in high Tec development in area fifty-four.

Since these flying disks existed knowingly, during the reign of Hitler and have been seen quite frequently during his time, I do not have to go on presenting you with more facts?

But I can still ask, "Are flying saucers or disks, if you like, real?"

According to millions of people, from all walks of life, who have seen, photographed, touched, built, were abducted, and chased these flying crafts, they will tell you that these flying machines are real. In fact, even the British Defense Ministry acknowledges that UFO'S exist..

## Dead Men are They Really Dead

They have released to the public, in October 2008, over 4,000 pages of UFO information. Needless to say, as expected, this covert information claims documented events of UFO sightings. But, are they really unidentified flying objects; or are they the covert high Tec flying discs of the west and of the east?

**e).  Dead Men are they Really Dead____** Are they really dead or are they alive?

Which is it?

As I have stated before, it took my mother almost twenty years to accept the fact that ghosts, demons, spirits, and apparitions are the products of Satan and his evil angels.

But regarding the zombies, I do not know if she accepted them as dead people walking around, once in a while, looking for their abusers in order to take vengeance upon them; or if she accepted the fact that the dead zombies were not really dead people but people who were drugged almost to a coma, in order to keep them alive and working in the fields and mines by some of the ruthless landlords. And whenever one or more of these zombies started to come out of their coma because the drug was not strong enough to sedate them anymore, they would come to town looking for their homes or go to unfamiliar places or to people they vaguely remember; and when they got there, people would be scared to death to see these zombies in their filthy and stinking conditions. It was well known fact; people who were afraid of their appearance shot many of the zombies. And when people found out who they shot, they questioned how could they have killed a dead person? And since there was no explanation found for their existence, many believed that the dead were coming back from their graves to take vengeance upon those who abused them.

But, what about real dead people, like the ones that are cremated or buried in their caskets, have you ever wondered if they are really dead?

Have you ever been in a third world country in a remote village? If you have, you would have noticed that the people of the village focus daily upon food, water, and shelter; and the rest of their needs are said to be a luxury. And one of their luxury needs is, what we call in the west, a witch doctor; but most of the places I have been to, they called the witch doctor "the healer."

Although these witch doctors are pretty good in what they do, in curing the sick, with their herbal medicines, most of the times, when they run out of their herbs, they go on long trips to find what they are looking for. And when they do, the people in the village are left without a doctor. When that happens, the people of the village are careful not to get sick, be bit by snakes, or get involved in accidents. If they do, they know that it will take many days before a witch doctor could come from a neighboring village to help them out. But when accidents do occur, like this one man who was bit by a poisonous snake on his hand, most people in the village knew what to do; therefore they manage to save other people's lives and even their own. But, when there is a more severe sickness taking hold upon one of the villagers, and the medicine man is not there to help the sick, by the time help comes, a person eventually dies because a person is too far gone in their ordeal. The medicine man is unable to help that person because he does not have the monitoring electronic gadgetry to reveal to him if the patient is getting better or worse. And because of the inability to monitor the changes effectively of a sick person that person dies—according to the modern standards, needlessly. And that's what happened in one of the villages.

After a long waited hope that the woman would recover from her sickness, the medicine man came out and said to the family that there was nothing more he could do for the sick woman. Not too long after, she passed away, and shortly after, she was made ready for her burial. And then, I, like everybody else, was asked to take part in the ceremonial death for the woman.

Notably, after the woman died, there was no autopsy performed to verify her death and to find out the cause of her death; instead there was a ceremonial death performed for the woman; and then, the body was put on display for the villagers to view and pay their respects. When the viewing was finished, the woman was taken to a burial place and laid to rest there amongst the many dead, which slept in their dusty field. And like the western and eastern beliefs, there was a ceremony performed for the good will of the woman's disembodied spirit. We were told that the people had to be kind to her disembodied spirit and to the family, in order for the sprit to find recognition and forgiveness for her evil deeds. And when

the spirit did find recognition and peace, the spirit would go into the Promised Land—wherever that was?
But because the majority of the villagers believed that sometimes the evil spirits, who do not want to leave planet earth, they influence the departed good spirits to turn evil and remain with them on earth. To ward off the evil spirits away from the woman's good departed spirit, the villagers, including the kids, tossed spears, stones, sticks, arrows, and some of them their knives way above the grave.
Although tossing knives over the grave was hazardous, at the end, it was more volatile claiming one's knife because there appeared, in events like these that there was always somebody claiming that he could not find his knife or someone else had it.
Nonetheless, I do not know if you have experienced the death of a person where there is no autopsy performed, no blood drained from the dead person's body, no organs removed to be donated, or makeup applied to his or her face and hands, in order to make a person look as if he or she was still alive and well; but I can assure you, there is a big difference between a natural unmolested dead body and a dressed up body in a funeral home. My experience has been and still is today that when we bury a body from a funeral home, it makes me feel that there is something missing, as if the dead person is not relay buried! But when I had viewed individuals buried in a third world country, I felt that all of that person was buried in the grave—he or she ceased to exist. They were gone. Perhaps I feel the difference so

*Ghosts Demons UFO'S and Dead Men*   By: Philip Mitanidis
**Dead Men are They Really Dead**

strongly because I have a tendency to think of how the funeral homes prepare a dead body and how they remove the blood from a dead person and inject into them toxic chemicals in their veins and how they remove organs to give to donors or covertly sell the organs to people with lots of money. Or perhaps it is just me?

In any case, one thing is very predominant in the eastern and western cultures, and that is the belief that when a person dies he or she sheds the fleshy body and gives up a spirit form (soul) of self and lives on forever in some realm somewhere. And some people in the east and west believe that the spirits (souls) of the dead go to heaven or to hell.

The majority of the eastern and western religious cultures will quickly agree that the conscious entity of a dead person is the "soul," many times referred to as the "spirit." But, when we asked, which entity is conscious, when a person is alive, the "spirit" or the "brain," people had difficult time differentiating between the two—especially in the third world countries. And when we asked who does the thinking and makes decisions, the spirit or the brain, many were perplexed? In fact, when the question was asked, if the "brain" was conscious, and if it had immortality, the majority did not know. And when people were asked, if the brain had immortality, when the brain was dead—brain dead—or barely functioning in a live person, again many were perplexed and could not give an answer. And when people were asked to reveal their immortal spirit (soul), many individuals became annoyed and shrugged off the question because they were not able to separate the soul from their body.

Although people from various faiths handled the above questions differently, they all, for one reason or another, still clung to their belief that a human being has an immortal soul; and at death that immortal soul moves on to a better place. But then again, some eastern religious cultures such as Hindus believe that the soul of a person does not necessarily move on to a better place of abode. They believe the disembodied soul could end up in a body of a lower form.

You see, a Hindu believer believes in "karma."

The basic belief that is taught about karma is that every act enforces a consequence; and that consequence can come in a negative or in a positive form. If the consequences upon a person are negative, due to his or her evil works in life and surpass the good works of that person, after his or her death, the soul will end up in a body that is lower than the human body. The soul could end up transporting itself into a donkey, a cow, a pig a frog, a bird, an insect, an worm, an elephant, a crow, and so on. And once the soul of the departed enters the lower form of a body that soul will strive to reach a higher level of existence after its shell dies. Or sometimes, believers might choose to stay in a lower form of a body, for whatever reason.

But those individuals who prefer to reach a higher state of existence, they will try to live a goodly life and perform certain rituals, as per the teaching of the Hindu doctrine, in order to transmigrate their soul into a higher plane of existence. And one of those daily rituals is to wash every morning in the Ganges River or in the local river. Although it is said that the Ganges River has the power to cleanse and purify the believers from all their sins, a wash in his or her home should still take place every morning, if the foregoing bodies of water are not accessible to the Hindu believer.

The fate of a Hindu's immortal soul is in his or her own hands. A person can make the immortal soul pass through many reincarnations by striving to attain a higher plane of existence to a point where the immortal soul finally sheds the multitudes of migrations of various body shells until it reaches a plane of peace and contentment in its spirit form. When a person's soul reaches that state, he or she is said to be set free (a state of "moksha").

So, in essence what the Hindu doctrine teaches is that an immortal soul occupies a baby at his or her birth and lives its life in good works or evil works, depending where the immortal soul wants to go to live next. The acceptance of that belief places the Hindu believer into a state of subordinate life that is why there are so many classes of people in India. It appears that they all accept their lot willingly and rejoice in someone's death, hopping that the dead person's soul moves on into a higher state of existence.

Having said that, how is it that Hindu believers do not know or recall their transmigrations, or if they have reached "moksha"? If a person's spirit transmigrates, should it not know where it has been?

The Buddhists have slightly different point of view

## Dead Men are They Really Dead

than the Hindus.

Although Buddhism derived from Hinduism, it teaches that man does not possess an immortal soul; and neither is man possessed by an immortal soul at birth or guided by an immortal soul. The followers of Buddhism believe in man's mental and physical forces to elevate the human body into a higher plateau of existence. And at the same time, Buddhism, like Hinduism, still believes that a human being wanders from life to life by rebirths. And the rebirths occur by the will, desire, choice, and by the preference of the human energy. Therefore it is stated that even though the body dies, these energies live on continually to produce a rebirth (re-existence).

The ultimate goal for the believer in the doctrine of Buddhism is to reach the state of enlightenment, salvation, and liberation from the human state. This state of liberation is identified as "Nirvana." Nirvana is not attained by the influence, or help, of some outside powers that are given to the individual; "Nirvana," it is believed, is attained by the powers that are within a person. Once "Nirvana" is reached, a person is said to have extinguished all passions and desires. He or she is said to be free from all sensory feelings, such as fear, love, desire, pain, hate, happiness, and so on.

But, when a person reaches a state of devoid sensory feelings, I wonder if a person is really in contentment?

How is a person going to know if he or she is content and in what state he or she are in, without the sensory feelings? And why would anyone want to be

## Dead Men are They Really Dead

annulled of his or her sensory feelings and emotions?

Do people really want to exist in a state of a coma?

Islam on the other hand teaches when man dies, his soul goes to heaven or to hell. This teaching can be found in the Qur'an, which is propagated by an individual called Muhammad.

Muhammad was born in a place called Mecca, Saudi Arabia, about 570 CE.

Muslims believe Muhammad is a prophet of Allah (God).

And in regards to the soul, contrary to the inspired Scriptures (Bible), the Muslims believe when a person dies his or her soul goes to paradise, a garden home, or to hell to be punished forever. But more precisely, Muslims believe that the soul goes to a place called "Barzakh" (a place of partition. Surah 23:99). The reason the souls end up in "Barzakh" is to wait for the judgment. Once the judgment is passed upon the soul, the soul is sent to one of the three places—paradise, garden home (Surah 4:57), or hell (Surah 7:38).

Hell in the Qur'an, for the soul, is described by Muhammad as follows:

> "54. Or are they jealous of mankind because of that which Allah of His bounty hath bestowed upon them? For We bestowed upon the house of Abraham (of old) the Scripture and wisdom, and We bestowed on them a mighty kingdom. 55. And of them were (some) who believed therein and of

them were (some) who disbelieved therein. Hell is sufficient for (their) burning.

"56. Lo! Those who disbelieve Our revelations, We shall expose them to the Fire. As often as their skins are consumed We shall exchange them for fresh skins that they may taste the torment. Lo! Allah is ever Mighty, Wise." Surah 4:54-56. (MMP)

"35. the reward of disbelievers is the Fire." Surah 13:35 (MMP)

As you have read in the above verses, the Qur'an teaches immortality contrary to the Bible. The Qur'an says that a person has an immortal soul. It states when the evil immortal souls are received by Allah, "42. at the time of their death." Surah 39:42 (MMP), the immortal souls are sent to hell to be tormented forever (Surah 4:54-56).

Since spirits do not have flesh, there is a contradiction in the Qur'an because the verse in Surah 4:56 states that the rebellious dead people's spirits will be given new skins every time the hell-fire burn them!

Since the Bible prophets of God do not teach that man is immortal and tormented forever and ever in hell, somewhere in Christ's universe, why is Muhammad further contradicting them by claiming that the opposite is true in Surah 4:54-56?

And, why is Muhammad saying that immortal man is tormented forever and ever? As per the meaning of the word immortal (impervious), an immortal soul or a person cannot be tormented, killed, or do him any harm; so how is an immortal soul or a person tormented in hell fire?

Furthermore, why is Muhammad contradicting Christ the LORD of hosts and His prophets when Christ says explicitly that the wicked men, women, Satan, and his evil angels will be "ashes" and "be no more"?

And since the Qur'an contradicts the Bible, on other doctrinal Bible subjects, why are the Muslims claiming that Muhammad is a prophet of the God of Abraham—especially when Muhammad and Muslims, like the Jews, do not worship the God of Abraham? I make the above statement because the Bible clearly says that the God of Abraham is Christ the LORD of hosts.

In the Jewish religion, some of the Jews during Christ's time, believed in the resurrection of the dead and some did not believe in the resurrection of the dead. But today, many Israelites lean towards the belief of the immortal soul doctrine. And ironically, not so much in hell because the Torah—in fact, the entire Old Testament does not teach eternal torment for the soul; it says, "the soul that sinneth it shall die" (Ezekiel 18:4).

Christians, on the other hand, today, like many eastern religions, believe contrary to the Bible doctrine; many claim that man possesses an immortal soul. They say that at death the soul goes to heaven or to hell. Although the New Testament, like the Old Testament, rejects the concept of an immortal soul, it should also be noted that both the Old and New Testaments reject the doctrine of eternal hell. There are no verses or a single verse, in the entire sixty-six books of the Bible, which supports the immortal soul doctrine or eternal hell.

Since that is a Biblical fact, why do Christians support and believe in immortal souls and eternal hell?

To answer, here are few references from the Bible, for your consideration that are commonly quoted out of context or misquoted, in order to support the immortal soul doctrine, sometimes identified as spirits or disembodied spirits.

But, before you read these verses, it should be noted that in all cases, the words immortal or immortality are added to the verse (s) by the immortality believers.

King Solomon wrote:

> "7 Then shall the dust return to the earth as it was: and the spirit shall return unto God who gave it." Ecclesiastes 12:7

Very convincing don't you think?

To further support the immortality doctrine, the spiritualist, like many Christians and none Christian religions, sight the death of Stephen in order to show that there is such a thing as a disembodied spirit.

The account reads, "47 But Solomon built Him an house. 48 Howbeit the most High dwelleth not in temples made with hands; as saith the prophet, 49 Heaven is My throne, and earth is My footstool: what house will ye build Me? saith the LORD: or what is the place of My rest? 50 Hath not My hand made all these things?

"51 Ye [all of you] stiffnecked and uncircumcised in heart and ears, ye [all of you] do always resist the Holy Ghost: as your fathers did, so do ye. 52 Which of the prophets have not your fathers persecuted? and they have slain them which shewed before of the coming of the Just One; of whom ye have been now the betrayers and murderers: 53 Who have received the law by the disposition of angels, and have not kept it.

"54 When they heard these things, they were cut to the heart, and they gnashed on him [Stephen] with their teeth. 55 But he, being full of the Holy Ghost, looked up steadfastly into heaven, and saw the glory of God, and Jesus standing on the right hand of God, 56 And said, Behold, I see the heavens opened, and the Son of man standing on the right hand of God. 57 Then they cried out with a loud voice, and stopped their ears, and ran upon him with one accord, 58 And cast him out of the city, and stoned him: and the witnesses laid down their clothes at a young man's feet, whose name was Saul [Apostle Paul]. 59 And they stoned Stephen, calling upon God, and saying, LORD Jesus, receive my spirit. 60 And he kneeled down, and cried with a loud voice, LORD, lay not this sin to their charge. And when he had said this, he fell asleep [died]." Acts 7:47-60

In addition to Stephen's statement (v.59), to further support the immortal soul doctrine, the spiritualists and Christians sight Christ's last words, which He uttered while hanging from Calvary's cross.

Christ's ordeal was as follows: "33 And when they were come to the place, which is called Calvary, there they

## Dead Men are They Really Dead

crucified Him [Christ], and the malefactors, one on the right hand, and the other on the left. 34 Then said Jesus, Father, forgive them; for they know not what they do. And they parted His raiment, and cast lots. 35 And the people stood beholding. And the rulers also with them derided Him, saying, He saved others; let Him save Himself, if He be Christ, the chosen of God. 36 And the soldiers also mocked Him, coming to Him, and offering Him vinegar, 37 And saying, If Thou be the king of the Jews, save Thyself. 38 And a superscription also was written over Him, in letters of Greek, and Latin, and Hebrew, THIS IS THE KING OF THE JEWS.

"39 And one of the malefactors which were hanged railed on Him, saying, If Thou be Christ, save Thyself and us. 40 But the other answering rebuked him, saying, Dost not thou fear God, seeing thou art in the same condemnation? 41 And we indeed justly; for we receive the due reward of our deeds: but this man hath done nothing amiss. 42 And he said unto Jesus, LORD, remember me when thou comest into Thy kingdom. 43 And Jesus said unto him, Verily I say unto thee, To day shalt thou be with me in paradise. 44 And it was about the sixth hour, and there was a darkness over all the earth until the ninth hour. 45 And the sun was darkened, and the veil of the temple was rent in the midst.

"46 And when Jesus had cried with a loud voice, He said, Father, into thy hands I commend My spirit: and having said thus, He gave up the ghost." Luke 23:33-46

As per verse forty-six, the believers in the immortal soul doctrine point out that it is obvious, like Stephen,

Christ's spirit departed from Him because Christ the LORD said, "into thy hands I commend My spirit."

And to further support their belief, the believers of the immortal soul doctrine state that while Christ was dead that weekend, He went, in His spirit form, to the disobedient disembodied human spirits of the antediluvians and preached to them.

To support their claim, they sight Peter's statement, which says,

> "18 For Christ also hath once suffered for sins, the just for the unjust, that He might bring us to God, being put to death in the flesh, but quickened by the Spirit: 19 By which also He went and preached unto the spirits in prison; 20 Which sometime were disobedient, when once the longsuffering of God waited in the days of Noah, while the ark was preparing, wherein few that is, eight souls were saved by water." 1 Peter 3:18-20

As you have read in the above verses, Solomon said, "7 Then shall the dust return to the earth as it was: and the spirit shall return unto God who gave it" (Ecclesiastes 12:7). And Stephen said, "59 LORD Jesus, receive my spirit" (Acts 7:59). And Jesus Christ the LORD of hosts said to the thief, who hung beside Him, "43 Verily I say unto thee [you], To day shalt thou [you] be with me in paradise" (Luke 23:43). And just before Jesus died, He said, "46 Father, into thy hands I commend My spirit: and having said thus, He gave up the ghost" (Luke

23:46). The above verses, it appears, are making serious claims about spirits leaving their bodies?

Do they?

But, let me ask you, "Did you read or see anywhere in the above verses the word 'immortality' or 'immortal'?"

Therefore, as per the above verses (Ecclesiastes 12:17; Acts 7:59; and Luke 23:46), do you really think that a human being has an "immortal" spirit, or an "immortal" soul, which leaves the body when he or she dies?

Obviously, as per the above verses, and like verses, which exist throughout the sixty-six books of the Bible, a spirit leaves the body, that much can be granted; and, as Solomon put it, "the spirit shall return unto God who gave it" (Ecclesiastes 12:7).

But before we go on, please keep in mind, nowhere do the above verses claim that the spirit, which leaves the body is man's immortal spirit.

Having made the above observation; don't get the idea that the prophets of the Bible support the immortal spirit (soul) doctrine, as the majority of the people throughout the world teach it. There is a reason why the above statements are made by King Solomon, Stephen, and by Jesus Christ the LORD.

Let me say again, throughout the Bible, the prophets of old, do not support the immortal soul (spirit) doctrine; and here is why: Let us begin with the prophet's input and with Christ's input, starting from Calvary's cross.

Just before Jesus died on Calvary's cross, Jesus said to one of the condemned men, who hung next to Him, he would be with Him in paradise.

Here is Christ's promise:

> "₄₃ And Jesus said unto him, Verily I say unto thee [you], To day shalt thou [you] be with me in paradise" (Luke 23:43).

Very convincing, don't you think?

So, what did Jesus mean?

Was the thief going to be that day in paradise, bodily with Christ the LORD of hosts, or was he going to be in a spirit form in paradise with Christ?

Well, according to the Bible, neither.

Here is why.

As you probably know, the Greeks, in ancient times, wrote their sentence structure in continues form and in capital letters. There was no space or punctuation marks between the words in a sentence. The punctuation marks and lower case letters are a modern injection into the Greek language. Therefore, if you are not fluent in the Greek language, you could very easily misunderstand the meaning of the sentence structures of the Gospel of Jesus Christ the LORD of hosts (Mark 1:1).

As an example, you can read the following sentence, HEISNOWHERE, couple of ways. You can say, "HE IS NOW HERE." Or you can say, "HE IS NOWHERE."

In another example, you cans say, MY AUNT SAID, "MY BROTHER, IS A LIER." Or you can say,

## Dead Men are They Really Dead

"MY AUNT," SAID MY BROTHER, "IS A LIER."

As you can plainly see in the above two examples, the meaning of the sentence is different when you rearrange the commas. Likewise, if the translators of the Greek text placed the comma after the words "To day," instead of "thee [you]," the meaning of Christ's statement would be different.

The verse would read,

> "43 And Jesus said unto him, Verily I say unto thee [you] To day, shalt thou [you] be with me in paradise" (Luke 23:43).

So, which statement is correct? "I say onto thee [you]," or "I say unto thee [you] To day"?

Since only God has immortality (1 Timothy 1:17; 6:13-16), and since there is not a single reference anywhere in the entire Bible, which states that man has immortality, a person has to conclude, the translators should have placed the comma after the words "To day," and not after the word "thee".

To further confirm the fact that the comma should have been placed after the words "To day," consider the following facts; on Sunday, the angel of the LORD said to the women at Christ's tomb, "6 Come, see the place where the LORD lay" (Matthew 28:6).

Jesus Christ the LORD was in the tomb from Friday to Sunday morning, He had not gone to paradise as the translators make the verse in Luke 23:43 to read. And to further confirm the fact that Jesus Christ did not go to paradise on Friday, Saturday, or Sunday, we have Christ's confirmation. When Mary met Jesus that Sunday morning, near His grave, He said to her, "17 Touch me not for I am not yet ascended to my Father" (John 20:17).

Therefore, if we were to accept Christ's own words that He had not ascended to paradise that Friday, Saturday, or Sunday, we can also conclude that the thief on the cross was not with Christ in a bodily form or in a spirit form on Friday on Saturday or on Sunday. There was no disembodiment of an immortal spirit soaring to paradise that Friday afternoon or roaming around the earth; but there were three dead people hanging on Calvary that late, late Friday afternoon who were oblivious to the hipped verbiage about them, of the scheming activities that were taking place by the authorities, and to the unceasing gossip, by the multitudes, of the current events that took place that weekend all around them.

According to the inspired Scriptures (Bible), Jesus Christ the LORD of hosts was resurrected on Sunday morning by God the Holy Spirit; but regarding the two thieves that were with Christ on Calvary, they were not resurrected into eternal life that weekend. There is no mention of their resurrection anywhere. Neither is there a verse, which states that one of the thieves that was promised eternal life that Friday afternoon, by Jesus Christ, was resurrected into eternal life.

Nonetheless, we can sight two more reasons why one of the thieves or the two thieves were not resurrected into eternal life that weekend; one, Jesus Christ the LORD of hosts was also dead during those three days.

And two, since Christ is the One who is going to resurrect the dead, at His second coming, it means that the two thieves were still dead during that weekend and are still dead today because Christ has not come the second time, as some would like us to believe, to resurrect the dead. The inescapable fact is that the dead are still dead. Therefore the two thieves are still dead today waiting for the resurrection of the just and for the resurrection of the damned to take place.

The two thieves, like everybody else that is dead, are dead and have decayed into the ground. They are oblivious to what is taking place around their surroundings, amongst the living, the universe, in heaven, and to their LORD God.

The prophet of the LORD makes the following two points about human beings; he says,

> "$_5$ the living know that they shall die: but the dead know not any thing neither have they any more a reward; for the memory of them is forgotten" (Ecclesiastes 9:5).

And the psalmist adds,

> "$_{17}$ The dead praise not the LORD, neither any that go down into silence [grave]." Psalms 115:17

Obviously, as per the above information that is

given to us by King Solomon and the psalmist, the dead are not alive, conscious, or praise the LORD.

But in order not to lose the argument that the dead are alive, and to substantiate their belief in the immortal soul (spirit) belief, they come back to Christ and Stephen and state that it is quite evident that Christ's spirit left His body that Friday afternoon because we are told that He went and "19 preached unto the spirits in prison."

Here are the verses:

> "18 For Christ also hath once suffered for sins, the just for the unjust, that He might bring us to God, being put to death in the flesh, but quickened [made alive] by the Spirit: 19 By which also he went and preached unto the spirits in prison; 20 Which sometime were disobedient, when once the longsuffering of God waited in the days of Noah, while the ark was preparing, wherein few that is, eight souls were saved by water." 1 Peter 3:18-20

Here are the above verses in the Greek text:

> "18 Επειδη και ο Χριστος απαξ επαθε δια τας αμαρτιας, ο δικαιος υπερ των αδικων, δια να φερη ημας προς τον Θεον, θανατωθεις μεν κατα την σαρκα, ζωοποιηθεις δε δια του Πνευματος 19 δια του οποιου πορευθεις εκηρυξε και προς τα πναυματα τα εν τη φηλακη" Πετρου Α 3:18, 19. Βιβλικη Εταιρεια 1961.

## Dead Men are They Really Dead

Another Greek text reads, "19 εν ω και τοις εν..." to indicate that the preaching to the antediluvians, by Noah, was done by the power of God the Holy Spirit.

As you can readily see in the Modern Greek text and in the old Greek text the words "By whom" is used to denote a reference to God the Holy Spirit of v.18. The words "By which" are not used in the Greek text as the King James Version of the Bibles states.

And to further confirm the fact that the word "whom" is used in v.19, here are vs.18 & 19 as they appear in the "New International Version" (NIV).

> "18 For Christ died for sins once for all, the righteous for the unrighteous, to bring you to God. He was put to death in the body but made alive by the Spirit. 19 Through whom also he went and preached to the spirits in prison." 1 Peter 3:18,19 (NIV)

So! According to the Greek text and the (NIV) Bible, Christ preached to the antediluvians by, or as the (NIV) puts it "through," God the Holy Spirit, before the deluge came upon those who were imprisoned spiritually by Satan during Noah's time. And the individual who was used by God the Holy Spirit to preach the Gospel message for one hundred and twenty years to the antediluvians, as you probably know, was Noah.

Please note: The verses state that it was the "Spirit" (God the Holy Spirit) that "quickened" (made Christ alive); and it was the "Spirit" (God the Holy Spirit) by whom or through "whom He [Christ] went and preached to the spirits [πνευμασι] in prison" during Noah's time.

So, to argue and base one's belief on the immortal spirit (soul) doctrine, on a mistranslated verse (v.19) of the King James Version of the Bible is futile. Just think about it, there is nothing that is said in the above verses about "immortality," "immortal souls," "immortal spirits" or Christ, during His death, two thousand years ago, who personally went to preach to dead spirits?

But more importantly, it should be noted in the above verses, it was not Christ who personally preached to the antediluvians; Apostle Peter states that Christ preached to the antediluvians by God the Holy Spirit before the flood came and swept them away. And that is a big difference.

On the other hand, if you want to assume that there are immortal spirits of the antediluvians hovering around somewhere and Christ singled them out for whatever reason, while He was dead, and went personally to "preach" to them only, and not to the rest of the dead, and you choose to base your faith on an assumption, remember that assumption becomes a personal opinion.

But, what about Christ's and Stephen's statements? The fact still remains; Jesus said:

> "46 Father, into thy hands I commend My spirit: and having said thus, He gave up the ghost." Luke 23:46

Stephen said:

> "⁵⁹ And they stoned Stephen, calling upon God, and saying, LORD Jesus, receive my spirit. ⁶⁰ And he kneeled down, and cried with a loud voice, LORD, lay not this sin to their charge. And when he had said this, he fell asleep [died]." Acts 7:59, 60

And King Solomon said:

> "⁷ Then shall the dust return to the earth as it was: and the spirit shall return unto God who gave it." Ecclesiastes 12:7

Very convincing—is it not?
Of course it is!
Since the above Scriptures state emphatically that there is a spirit that is commended in the hands of God the Father by Jesus Christ; and that there is a spirit, which is commended to Jesus Christ by Stephen, a person has to conclude as such.

But, if that is the case, why does Job state that he will see God (Christ) at His second coming, and not when he dies?

Here is his statement:

> "²⁵ For I know that my Redeemer liveth, and that He shall stand at the latter day upon the earth: ²⁶ And though after my skin worms destroy this body, yet in my flesh shall I see God" (Job 19:25, 26).

## Dead Men are They Really Dead

So! Is there an answer?

Obviously there is, since the prophets of the inspired Scriptures do not contradict each other, there is an answer.

Consider the following: When Adam was created from the dust of the ground by Jesus Christ the LORD of hosts, Adam was a lifeless composition of various molecular earthly structures (atoms). In order to bring this lifeless human form into life, we are told that Christ blew into Adam's nostrils the "breath of life."

Here is the account:

> "7 And the LORD God formed man of the dust of the ground, and breathed into his nostrils the breath of life; and man became a living soul." Genesis 2:7

Thus, according to the above verse, the "breath of life" and a body of flesh equals to a "living soul."

So! What does the breath of life consist of?

According to the prophet of old, he says that "the breath of life" consist of the "spirit of God" and a "breath" (oxygen).

Here is his statement:

> "4 The spirit of God hath made me, and the breath of the Almighty hath given me life" (Job 33:4).

The "spirit of God" is the sustaining life force, which not only sustains the human race but it is the life force that sustains the whole creation and everything that is in it. We are told, "₄ In Him [Christ] was life" and "₁₇ by Him [Christ] all things consist" (John 1:4; Colossians 1:17). In fact, the "heavens and the earth, which are now," they were created by Jesus Christ the LORD of hosts; and they are kept by His word in their orbits, as the above verse (v.17) states and as Peter the prophet of the LORD agrees with Apostle Paul. He says,

> "₆ Whereby the world [antediluvians] that then was, being overthrown with water, perished:
>
> "₇ But the heavens and the earth, which are now, by the same word are kept in store, reserved unto fire against the day of judgment and perdition of ungodly men" (2 Peter 3:6, 7).

Thus, as per the above verses, the universe and the life force in a person is sustained by the word of Christ the Creator.

And regarding the "breath," which leaves a deceased person, as Moses stated before, it is the oxygen we breathe.

If a person loses his or her breath and clinically dies, it does not mean that he or she will die. There are many clinical reports where people have been clinically pronounced dead and to the doctor's surprise, later on, they recover.

There are clinical reports where some people were dead for many minutes. In fact there are reports where some people have been clinically dead for twenty minutes and revived. And those who revived have given many testimonies regarding their death experience. Some have stated that they saw, in a bright light, people acting in various scenarios; but almost all have stated that they observed a very bright light, which surrounded them. Because of these types of experiences, and ignorance to the inspired Scriptures (Bible), many who were clinically dead, have stated that they were out of the body. What these individuals have failed to understand is the fact that it was the "spirit" (the life giving force of God that sustained them). If the "spirit" was removed by God, as Scripture has stated, those individuals who died clinically, for a number of minutes, would not be able to experience the effects of the bright light. But because God chose to extend their lives, for whatever reason, they had the experience of the bright light and revived.

Although there is a great debate about the bright light, which the clinically dead people see, the bottom line about this light is the sustaining power of the "spirit of God" who allows the neurons of the brain to continue to fire their electric currents throughout the brain, in order for the brain to revive the body into proper function.

But, if the "spirit of God" (life source) was removed from these clinically dead people, they would have died right away.

Therefore as long as we have the "spirit" (life force of God) and the "breath" (oxygen) in us, like Job (Job 27:3), we can work, play, entertain, read, etc., etc.

But, if God decides to "[14] gather unto Himself His

spirit and His breath; ₁₅ All flesh shall perish together, and man shall turn again unto dust" (Job 34:14, 15).

King Solomon agrees with what Job is saying; Solomon says that the "₇ spirit shall return unto God who gave it" (Ecclesiastes 12:7).

As a result, when Jesus Christ the LORD said "₄₆ Father, into thy hands I commend My spirit: and having said thus, He gave up the ghost [exhaled εξεπναυσεν]" (Luke 23:46); and Stephen's statement, when he said, "₅₉ LORD Jesus, receive my spirit" (Acts 7:59), what they were doing is the fact that they both knew that they were going to die at any moment; therefore they each commended the "spirit of God" (life source) that was given to them back to God who gave it.

Thus, Solomon's statement, which says, "₇ Then shall the dust return to the earth as it was: and the spirit shall return unto God who gave it" (Ecclesiastes 12:7) is correct.

In conclusion then, "the breath of life," which was inserted into Adam's nostrils (Genesis 2:7), by Christ the LORD, consisted of the "the spirit" (life source), which belongs to Christ, and the "breath" (oxygen), which Adam began to breath after the "spirit" of Christ was placed in him.

So, to argue that a man is an immortal being by using the examples of Christ and Stephen is futile because the prophet of the LORD says that man does not have immortality, only God has immortality.

Here is his statement.

"₁₅ Which in his [God the Father's] times he

shall shew, who is the blessed and only Potentate, the King of kings, and Lord of lords; 16 Who only hath immortality, dwelling in the light which no man can approach unto; whom no man hath seen, nor can see: to whom be honour and power everlasting. Amen." 1 Timothy 6:15, 16

By the way, why are believers in the immortal soul doctrine quoting Ecclesiastes 12:7 to support their belief that man has an intelligent immortal soul that returns to God? Don't they realize that they make all good and evil souls or spirits soar to God and none descending to hell?

The verse defeats their claim!

Now we can ask, "According to the Bible, what happens to a person when he or she dies?"

According to the Bible, we are told that

"5 the living know that they shall die: but the dead know not anything,"

Did you hear that?

We are told, "the dead know not anything." And then, the prophet of the LORD adds, "neither have they any more a reward; for the memory of them is forgotten. 6 Also their love, and their hatred, and their envy, is now perished: neither have they any more a portion for ever in any thing that is done under the sun."

Therefore, King Solomon adds,

"¹⁰ Whatsoever thy hand findeth to do, do it with thy might; for there is no work, nor device, nor knowledge, nor wisdom, in the grave, whither thou [you] goest" (Ecclesiastes 9:5, 6, 10).

In fact, Solomon says that "²⁰ All go unto one place; all are of the dust, and all turn to dust" (Ecclesiastes 3:20).

Likewise, the psalmist says the same thing.

"⁴ His breath goeth forth, he returneth to his earth; in that very day his thoughts perish" (Psalms 146:4).

So, what is death like in the grave?

According to Jesus Christ the LORD of hosts who created man says that death in the grave is like sleep.

Here are His words;

"¹¹ These things said He [Christ]: and after that He said unto them [His disciples], Our friend Lazarus sleepeth; but I go, that I may awake him out of sleep. "¹² Then said His disciples, LORD, if he sleep, he shall do well. "¹³ Howbeit Jesus spake of his death: but they thought that He had spoken of taking of rest in sleep" (John 11:11-13).

According to the above verses, all human beings, good or evil, saved for Christ's kingdom or not, are in a state of unconsciousness in the grave. And the only time they are going to be awakened is when Jesus Christ the LORD of hosts resurrects them into consciousness, or calls them out of their sleep, if you like, to life again.

Here are the references:

> "28 Marvel not at this: for the hour is coming, in the which all that are in the graves shall hear His voice. 29 And shall come forth; they that have done good, unto the resurrection of life; and they that have done evil, unto the resurrection of damnation" (John 5:28, 29).

Did you notice the word "all" in v.28?

We are told, "all" of the dead people, "good" and "evil," are in their graves waiting to be resurrected. Christ says, "all that are in the graves shall hear His voice," and when they do, they will be resurrected into life.

Did you also notice in verse twenty-nine what Christ the LORD of hosts said?

He said that there are two resurrections. There is a resurrection of the "good," which will be resurrected into eternal life; and there is a resurrection of the "evil" men and women, which will be resurrected into "damnation."

So! When will the resurrection of all the dead righteous ("good") men, women, and children going to take place?

According to Christ's own words, the resurrection of the righteous will take place at His second coming.

Here is His promise:

"₁ LET not your heart be troubled: ye [all of you] believe in God, believe also in Me. ₂ In My Father's house are many mansions: if it were not so, I would have told you. I go to prepare a place for you. ₃ And if I go and prepare a place for you, I will come again, and receive you unto Myself; that where I am, there ye may be also" (John 14:1-3).

When will the above event take place?
According to Christ the LORD of hosts, the above event will take place "Immediately after the tribulation."

Here is the account: "₂₉ Immediately after the tribulation of those days [Revelation chapter 16] shall the sun be darkened, and the moon shall not give her light, and the stars shall fall from heaven, and the powers of the heavens shall be shaken: ₃₀ And then shall appear the sign of the Son of man in heaven: and then shall all the tribes of the earth mourn, and they shall see the Son of man coming in the clouds of heaven with power and great glory. ₃₁ And He [Christ] shall send His angels with a great sound of a trumpet, and they shall gather together His elect from the four winds, from one end of heaven to the other." Matthew 24:29-31

And according to Apostle John, the second coming of Jesus Christ the LORD of hosts, and of the resurrection of the righteous ("good"), will take place in between the sixth and seventh plague that is described in Revelation chapter sixteen.

But before the second coming of Jesus Christ takes place, you should be informed prophetically about the super bugs, pandemics, unstoppable fires, famines, pestilences, earthquakes, sores, viruses, boils, and of the extreme erratic deadly unheard of weather patterns that will continue to escalate throughout the world, due to the stressful harm man has imposed upon the ecosystem.

On top of that list, there will be shortages of drinking water, food, and energy, due to the constant destruction of the earth's ecosystem and ozone depletion.

In addition, there will be extreme labor unrest, usury, slavery, prostitution, abandonment of senior citizens, abandonment of children, child labor, child prostitution, crime, wars, and roomers of wars, etc., etc.

Although the above extreme weather, volcano activities, earthquakes, famine, labor, crime, food riots, wars, diseases, death decree upon Christ's Covenant Keepers, and the cost of food, water, and energy will continuously escalate, they are no comparison to the seven last plagues, which will create havoc, misery, pain, hunger, death, lunacy, lawlessness, and destructive convulsion of the earth, after Christ utters the words,

> "11 He that is unjust, let him be unjust still: and he which is filthy, let him be filthy still: and he that is righteous, let him be righteous still: and he that is holy: let him be holy still" (Revelation 22:11).

## Dead Men are They Really Dead

Once the above decree is uttered by Christ the LORD of hosts, the catastrophic seven last plagues will erupt upon the evil inhabitants of the earth and avoid Christ's Covenant keepers (Revelation 18:4). As the seven last plagues fall upon the wicked and upon the ecosystem, they will add to the super bugs, diseases, pain, death, lawlessness, uprising, extreme weather patterns, earth quakes, fires, floods, scorching, and cause the earth to go into extreme convulsions throughout the world.

To give you a brief overview of Christ's second coming, and of the prophetic events that will take place at His coming, here is a modified excerpt (Bible quotations expanded) taken from the book "Christians Headed Into the Time of Trouble *By: Philip Mitanidis,*" starting from Revelation chapter sixteen and verse seventeen.

> "17 And the seventh angel poured out his vial into the air; and there came a great voice out of the temple of heaven, from the throne, saying, It is done" (Rev 16:17).
>
> As you have read in verse seventeen above, God the Father, as we know him now, in the New Testament, utters the words from Christ's throne, "It is done." When God the Father utters the words "It is done," it means that he has put all of Christ's "enemies under His feet." And when God the Father has done that, he then relinquishes his position as an overseer of Christ's universe and everything that is in it and outside of it.
>
> Here is the reference: "24 Then cometh the end, when he shall have delivered up the kingdom to God, even the Father: when he shall have put down all rule and all authority and power. 25 For he must reign, till he hath put all enemies under His feet [Christ's feet. See Psalms 110:1;

Hebrews 1:8]" (1 Corinthians 15:24, 25).

By the way, I do not want to go into lot of explanation regarding v.24; but simplistically, the words "even the" do not exist in the Greek Scriptures; the word in the Greek is "και," which translates in English into the coordinating conjunction "and." Therefore, to clarify v.24, it will read as follows: "24 Then cometh the end, when he [God the Father] shall have delivered up the kingdom to God and Father [Christ]: when he [God the Father] shall have put down all rule and all authority and power. 25 For he [God the Father of vs. 15, 24] must reign, till he [God the Father] hath put all enemies under His feet [Christ's feet]" (1 Corinthians 15:24, 25).

Once God the Father hands over Christ's kingdom (universe) to Christ the LORD of hosts, Christ the LORD of hosts begins to reign again and prepares to come to planet earth, at the beginning of the seventh plague, with His angels (saints), to gather His people who are alive and those who are dead.

As Christ the LORD of hosts approaches planet earth with His holy angels (saints), the birds will be feeding upon the abundant "carcases." "28 wheresoever the carcase is, there will the eagles be gathered together." And as Christ and His angels come closer, "29 Immediately after the tribulation of those days shall the sun be darkened, and the moon shall not give her light, and the stars shall fall from heaven, and the powers of the heavens shall be shaken: 30 and then shall appear the sign of the Son of man in heaven: and then shall all the tribes of the earth mourn, and they shall see the Son of man coming in the clouds of heaven with power and great glory" (Matthew 24:28-30).

As the above overwhelming long waited event takes place, for many, the scene becomes a terrifying and hateful view; but none can escape it. And, as some people gaze at the scene and some run to hide, there will be additional devastating events taking place. The prophet of the LORD explains, "18 And there were voices, and thunders, and lightnings; and there was a great earthquake, such as was not since men were upon the earth, so mighty an earthquake, and so great. 19 And the great city [Vatican] was divided into three parts, and the cities of the nations fell; and great Babylon came in remembrance before God, to give unto her the cup of the wine of the fierceness of His wrath" (Revelation 16:18, 19).

And when Christ reaches planet earth visibly with His holy angels and park themselves in the sky, above planet earth, Christ will illuminate planet earth from the east to the west (Matt 24:27), as it revolves on its axes, so that every eye will be able to see them (Revelation 1:7). And when they see Christ and His holy angels, Christ's Covenant keepers will rejoice; but the ungodly will scramble in fear and try to hide from Christ the LORD.

Apostle Paul adds, "8 And then shall that Wicked be revealed, whom the LORD shall consume with the spirit of His mouth, and shall destroy with the brightness of His coming" (2 Thessalonians 2:8).

In addition, "15 the kings of the earth, and the great men, and the rich men, and the chief captains, and the mighty men, and every bondman, and every free man, hid themselves in the dens and in the rocks of the mountains: 16 And said to the mountains and rocks, Fall on us, and hide us from the face of Him that sitteth on the throne, and from the wrath of the Lamb: 17 For the great day of His wrath is come; and who shall be able to stand?" (Revelation 6:15-17).

Obviously, the ungodly know who has come with full power and glory to gather His elect. They know because they have heard the messages of the three angels; that is why the ungodly call for the rocks and mountains to fall upon them. But the rocks and mountains do not move for them. They know that they will suffer the consequences, which they had chosen.

As the ungodly scatter to hide from Christ the LORD of hosts, Christ calls forth the righteous dead from the graves"

**Apostle Paul explains:** "51 Behold, I [Apostle Paul] shew you a mystery; We shall not all sleep [be dead], but we shall all be changed. 52 In a moment, in the twinkling of an eye, at the last trump: for the trumpet shall sound, and the dead shall be raised incorruptible, and we shall be changed. 53 For this corruptible must put on incorruption, and this mortal must put on immortality. 54 So when this corruptible shall have put on incorruption, and this mortal shall have put on immortality, then shall be brought to pass the saying that is written [Hosea 13:14], Death is swallowed up in victory" (1 Corinthians 15:51-54)."

At that moment, when "death is swallowed up in victory," Christ the LORD of hosts "gives them [the righteous] a new youthful glorious body without blemish, like unto His own body"

Here is the reference: "20 For our conversation is in heaven; from whence also we look for the Saviour, the LORD Jesus Christ; "21 Who shall change our vile body, that it may be fashioned like unto His glorious body, according to the working whereby He is able even to subdue all things unto Himself" (Philippians 3:20, 21).

"And as the righteous dead rise in youthful bodies, from their graves of land and sea, amongst the cataclysmic destruction of the earth, Christ's Covenant keepers and the resurrected look up towards heaven with overwhelming joy and contentment to see their LORD God and Savior waiting to deliver them from their enemies.

And as they wait, they see Christ's holy angels flying

down to earth and taking His holy people up in the sky where Christ is stayed. The record states, "31 And He [Christ] shall send His angels with a great sound of a trumpet, and they shall gather together His elect from the four winds, from one end of heaven to the other." "40 Then shall two be in the field; the one shall be taken, and the other left. 41 Two women shall be grinding at the mill; the one shall be taken, and the other left" (Matthew 24:31, 40, 41). Thus fulfilling the apostle's prophetic words that the righteous dead will not go to heaven before the living."

**Here is the reference:** "39 And these all, having obtained a good report through faith, received not the promise: 40 God having provided some better thing for us, that they [the righteous dead] without us [the righteous living] should not be made perfect" (Hebrews 11:39, 40).

"As the sky swells with the redeemed, the redeemed look down upon the earth and recall, in a pitiful way, the horrors of what sin has done to the planet and to the human race.

And when all of the redeemed are gathered from the four corners of the earth, Christ the LORD of hosts, His angels, and the redeemed start their journey towards the third heaven to be with Christ the LORD. (See John 14:3; Rev. 21:7.)"

So! While Christ the LORD of hosts and the redeemed travel towards the third heaven, what happens on earth to the wicked men and women during the seventh plague?

"Now that the earth is not protected by God; the ungodly realize that they are left behind and not saved. In their raging anxiety, with agony and fierce passion, the ungodly turn their mad evil frustration upon those individuals, who deceived them. In relentless anger and rage, the ungodly who were deceived by the politicians, priests, clergy, Imams, rabbis, theologians, Bible teachers, pastors, those who suppressed them, and those individuals who abused them, they seek them out and fall violently upon them to kill them  Thus the ungodly fall to the left and to the right, in unmerciful bloodshed throughout the world.

Meanwhile, as Christ, His angels, and the redeemed move away from the earth, the disturbance of their movements, in space, cause the magnetic field of the earth to stress, go off course, and go into convulsion of unseen and unheard of proportions. The prophet of the LORD explains, "20 every island fled away, and the mountains were not found. 21 And there fell upon men a great hail out of heaven, every stone about the weight of a talent [64 lbs.]: and men blasphemed God because of the plague of the hail; for the plague thereof was exceeding great" (Revelation 16:20, 21).

And Jeremiah adds, "32 Thus saith the LORD of hosts, Behold, evil shall go forth from nation to nation, and great whirlwind shall be raised up from the coasts of the earth. 33 And the slain of the LORD shall be at that day from one end of the earth even unto the other end of the earth: they shall not be lamented, neither gathered, nor buried, they shall be dung [animal shit] upon the ground" (Jeremiah 25:32, 33).

The devastation of the earth and bloodshed of man and beast, due to the plagues and the anger of the deceived and of the oppressed, leave the human carcasses all over the world unburied because there will be no human soul alive to bury all of the dead; instead, for a short period of time, so some of the surviving birds of the air will have a feast upon all of the dead carcasses.

The prophet of the LORD says,

"33 the slain of the LORD shall be at

that day from one end of the earth even unto the other end of the earth: they shall not be lamented, neither gathered, nor buried, they shall be dung upon the ground" (Jeremiah 25:33).

In reference to the destruction of the earth's ecosystem, man, and beast, the LORD foretold Satan's demolition of the planet and man. The LORD said to Satan (Lucifer), "20 Thou [you] shalt not be joined with them [unrighteous dead] in burial, because thou hast destroyed thy land, and slain thy people: the seed [offspring] of evildoers shall never be renowned" (Isaiah 14:20).

Shortly after the above destructive impact upon the earth, by the seventh plague, the earth will further destabilize and start swinging, to and fro like a drunkard. And on top of all that, the sun will stop shining.

The prophet of the LORD explains,

"19 The earth is utterly broken down, the earth is clean dissolved, the earth is moved exceedingly. 20 The earth shall reel to and fro like a drunkard, and shall be removed like a cottage; and the transgression thereof shall be heavy upon it; and it shall fall, and not rise again" (Isaiah 24:19, 20).

As the earth moves in its destructive form, to and fro like a "drunkard," in the frigid dark space, there will be no human, animal, fish, or bird left alive on or in the planet." ____[1]

---

[1]  Mitanidis Philip, *Christians Headed Into the Time of Trouble*, BeeHive Publishing house Inc. 2007

Since the righteous dead and righteous living are taken to the third heaven to be with Christ the LORD, and the wicked are all dead on earth, what happens to Satan and to his evil angels?

While Satan and his evil angels manage to a large degree to avoid death during the second coming of Christ the LORD of hosts and during the seven last plagues, regarding Satan, the LORD said that Satan will not see death during the time of the plagues; he will not be buried with the "evil" dead men and women.

Here is the reference;

> "[20] Thou [you] shalt not be joined with them in burial, because thou hast destroyed thy land, and slain thy people: the seed [offspring] of evildoers shall never be renowned" (Isaiah 14:20).

Satan and his evil angels who have deceived, terrorized, perverted, maimed, diseased, and destroyed billions upon billions of people on planet earth will find themselves all alone on the dark frigid planet earth, swinging to and fro like a drunkard, as it orbits endlessly around its unstable dead sun, for one thousand years.

Here are the references:

> "[1] AND I saw and angel come down from heaven, having the key of the bottomless pit and a great chain in his hand.

> "2 And he laid hold on the dragon, that old serpent, which is the Devil, and Satan, and bound him a thousand years,
>
> "3 And cast him into the bottomless pit, and shut him up, and set a seal upon him, that he should deceive the nations no more, till the thousand years should be fulfilled: and after that he must be loosed a little season" (Revelation 20:1-3).

Therefore, Satan and his evil angels will find themselves all alone on and in our frozen earth in a bitter and frustrating circumstances, which will drive them to scurry for survival and plunge his terrorizing rule into further malice and bitter anarchy amongst his evil angels.

Life for Satan and his evil angels will not be so sweet after all because during the one thousand years there will be no human, bird, or animal alive to tempt, deceive, or toy with, as he had done in the past. (Jeremiah 25:33; Isaiah 24:19, 20.)

So, while Satan and his evil angels are chained circumstantially for one thousand years, on the dark frozen, and broken down planet earth, what happens, at that period of time, to all of the wicked dead men and women that are on planet earth?

We are told that "5 the rest of the dead lived not again until the thousand years were finished" (Rev. 20:5).

According to the above verse, after the devastating destruction of the earth takes place by the seventh plague

(Revelation 16:17), all of the wicked dead men and women will remain dead for one thousand years. The verse reads, "₅ the rest of the dead lived not again until the thousand years were finished" (Revelation 20:5). And when the wicked are resurrected at the end of the one thousand years; that resurrection of the wicked would be their first resurrection—but then again, not for all of the wicked dead.

Let me clarify the above statement; for the majority of the wicked dead men and women, according to Revelation 20:5, would be the first resurrection, but for some of the wicked dead, as per Revelation 1:7, it would be their second resurrection.

Here is the account:

> "₇ Behold He [Christ] cometh in clouds; and every eye shall see Him, and they also which pierced Him: and all kindreds of the earth shall wail because of Him. Even so, Amen" (Revelation 1:7).

As it is stated in the above verse, there will be a special resurrection, at the second coming of Christ the LORD of hosts, for those individuals who pierced Christ the LORD of hosts, during the time He hung on the cross that Friday afternoon two thousand years ago, in order to see if Christ was dead or not? And there will be a special resurrection for those individuals who nailed Christ's hands and feet on the rugged cross. And more likely, even Caiaphas the high priest, the elders, scribes, those who spit on Him, those who whipped Him, those who beat Him, those who mocked Him, those individuals who pulled His beard, those who voted to crucify Him, etc., etc., will be resurrected from their deathbeds during Christ's second coming. (Daniel 12:1, 2; Matt. 26:47-68.)

But, regardless to which wicked men and women are referred to in Revelation 1:7, and who is going to be resurrected, during Revelation 1:7, they will all suffer the outpouring of the seventh plague and die with the rest of the wicked at that time, and remain dead for one thousand years on our frozen dark earth (Rev. 20:5).

During the one thousand years period, our earth will look like the way the earth was before Christ the LORD of hosts created the moon, the sun, the ecosystem of the earth, and man.

We are told, "2 the earth was without form, and void; and darkness was upon the face of the deep" (Genesis 1:2).

Nonetheless, regardless of which resurrection the wicked men and women are going to be brought forth, according to John 5:29, they will all be brought forth "unto the resurrection of damnation."

So! When will the first resurrection, which will be the second for some of the wicked dead, take place?

According to Revelation twenty and verses five and thirteen, the first resurrection of the wicked men and women will take place at the end of the one thousand years.

"5 But the rest of the dead lived not again

until the thousand years were finished. This is the first resurrection" (Revelation 20:5).

When the one thousand years are expired, all of the wicked men and women will be resurrected to life. They will all rise from their graves with the same evil attitude they went into the graves—mortal, naked, deformed, and in their old degenerate condition in which they all originally went into their graves.
The prophet of the LORD says,

"$_{13}$ And the sea gave up the dead which were in it; and death and hell [grave] delivered up the dead which were in them: and they were judged every man according to their works" (Revelation 20:13).

When the wicked dead men and women rise from their deathbeds, they will notice each other's naked, mortal, and horrifying degenerate condition. Everywhere they look, they will see a sea of naked human bodies and the endless destruction of the ruined dismal earth. And when they see each other's faces, they will observe the horror of what sin has done to them mentally and physically. Then, they will ponder why they are all naked? And as they interact with each other and ask thousand upon thousand of questions, they will wonder what is their lot? And as they search for answers, eventually, they will notice a bright light emanating from one corner of planet earth! And that corner is Mount Moriah. The reason there would be a bright light emanating from

Mount Moriah is due to the fact that New Jerusalem and the redeemed, after the one thousand years are expired, would have come down from heaven and settled upon it.

The prophet of the LORD says,

> "2 And I John saw the holy city, new Jerusalem, coming down from God out of heaven, prepared as a bride adorned for her husband" (Revelation 21:2).

As news spreads around the globe amongst the resurrected wicked dead men and women that New Jerusalem has come down from heaven and it is occupied by the redeemed, they all wonder what comes next, or more precisely, if there is any hope for them; and if they should go and join them? But to their surprise, when Satan sees the human sea of the naked and deformed masses bumping into each other endlessly, he and his evil angels excite the wicked to declare war upon New Jerusalem and upon its occupants. He tells them, if they do not go and overtake the holy city, they will all perish.

They all look around planet earth, and see the endless sea of human degenerate flesh and realize that the earth, in its broken down condition, it cannot sustain them; therefore they all rally around Satan and his evil angels, and thrust themselves forward towards the holy city.

The record says,

> "7 And when the thousand years are expired,

Satan shall be loosed out of his prison. 8 And shall go out to deceive the nations which are in the four corners of the earth, God and Magog, to gather them together to battle: the number of whom is as the sand of the sea" (Revelation 20:8).

As Satan gathers and leads the wicked to the holy city, Christ the LORD of hosts appears above the earth in blazing glory and stops the intruders in their tracks.

As they look up and gaze at Christ the LORD of hosts, Christ passes judgment upon them. When judgment is passed upon them, the wicked men, women, Satan, and his evil angels reflect upon their panoramic life with all the good and evil acts they had committed.

Once they recollect their life's history and how they mockingly used to say, "14 unto God, Depart from us; for we desire not the knowledge of thy ways" (Job 21:14), and how they "12 had pleasure in unrighteousness" (2 Thessalonians 2:12), and refused to accept eternal salvation through Jesus Christ the LORD, and chose the path of evil, they realize that there is no hope for salvation, and that they have reached the end of their lustful evil journey. In their helpless state, they all fall down on their knees and acknowledge that Jesus Christ the LORD of hosts is the God of His universe and everything that is in it.

Here is their acknowledgement:

"11 For it is written, As I live, saith

> the LORD, every knee shall bow to me, and every tongue shall confess to God" (Romans 14:11).

After they all acknowledge their rebellious sinful state and that Christ the LORD of hosts is the LORD God of His universe, they also realize that their pending doom is at hand. That realization sparks resentment towards Christ the LORD and unleashes, from their evil hearts, the hate they all have for Christ the LORD of hosts (Exodus 20:5; Luke 6:22; Rev. 12:17). As their hate surfaces violently towards Christ, for not letting them continue to live their sinful lives on planet earth, they make one last effort to overtake the holy city. In maddening rage and fury, Satan, his evil angels, men, and women, try to enter into the city of New Jerusalem.

The prophet of the LORD says,

> "9 they went up on the breadth of the earth, and compassed the camp of the saints about, and the beloved city; and fire came down from God out of heaven, and devoured them 10 And the devil that deceived them was cast into the lake of fire and brimstone, where the beast and the false prophet are, and shall be tormented day and night for ever and ever" (Revelation 20:9, 10). "14 And death and hell [grave] were cast into the lake of fire. This is the second death. 15 And whosoever was not found written in the book of life was cast into the lake of fire" (Revelation 20:14, 15).

As you have read in the above verses (Rev. 20:9, 10), planet earth will be turned into a "lake of fire."

In verse ten of Revelation twenty, if you read the Greek text, you will find that it says that Satan threw himself into the lake of fire; he like the rest of the wicked men and women were not pushed into it. The LORD'S desire, all along has been that none should perish (2 Peter 3:9); but perish they will because knowingly, the wicked chose their eternal demise in "the lake of fire" in stead of eternal youthful immorality in Christ's kingdom.

In reference to the coming inferno (lake of fire), the prophet of the LORD says,

> "₇ But the heavens and the earth, which are now, by the same word are kept in store, reserved unto fire against the day of judgment and perdition of ungodly men."

> "₉ The LORD is not slack concerning His promise, as some men count slackness; but is longsuffering to us-ward, not willing that any should perish, but that all should come to repentance.

> "₁₀ But the day of the LORD will come as a thief in the night; in the which the heavens shall pass away with a great noise, and the elements shall melt with fervent heat, the earth also and the works that are therein shall be burned up.

> "₁₁ Seeing then that all these things shall be dissolved, what manner of persons ought ye to be in all holy conversation and godliness,
>
> "₁₂ Looking for and hasting unto the coming of the day of God, wherein the heavens being on fire shall be dissolved, and the elements shall melt with fervent heat?" 2 Peter 3:7, 9-12

If the warning is not headed by the wicked, before the seven plagues start to fall upon them and upon the ecosystem of the earth, we are told that the wicked "will be consumed."

> "₂₀ But the wicked shall perish, and the enemies of the LORD shall be as the fat of lambs: they shall consume; into smoke shall they consume away" (Psalms 37:20).

The wicked will "consume away" into smoke because the final result of the wicked will be "ashes."

> "₁ FOR, behold, the day cometh, that shall burn as an oven; and all the proud, yea, and all that do wickedly, shall be stubble: and the day that cometh shall burn them up, saith the LORD of host, that it shall leave them neither root nor branch.
>
> "₃ And ye shall tread down the wicked; for they shall be ashes under the soles of your feet in the

day that I shall do this, saith the LORD of hosts" (Malachi 4:1, 3)

.   As you have read in the above verses, when the wicked are consumed (man and evil angels), and turned into "ashes" that will be their "second death" (Revelation 20:14). Not only the wicked will be burned to "ashes," by the inferno, but, the very elements of the earth and the surrounding area will be ignited into lava. The prophet of the LORD says that the "heavens" "shall be dissolved" and the very "elements shall melt with fervent heat?" He explains:

> "10 in the which the heavens shall pass away with a great noise, and the elements shall melt with fervent heat, the earth also and the works that are therein shall be burned up.
>
> "12 Looking for and hasting unto the coming of the day of God, wherein the heavens being on fire shall be dissolved, and the elements shall melt with fervent heat?" 2 Peter 3:10, 12

The reason the inferno will be ignited upon the earth and vicinity is simply to purify planet earth, space, and the local planets from the contamination of sin and sinner. Wherever and in whomever sin is found, the fire will burn it, as long as it takes, and purify the space it occupies.

It should be noted, if sin is accumulated within a

person, it is accumulated because that person did not want Christ to forgive his or her sins; therefore that person will burn in the fire because sin dwells within him or her. The amount of time that person will burn, in the fire, will depend upon the degree that person has accumulated sin in his or her life. If an individual has accumulated small amount of sin in his or her life that person will burn less than the individual who has large amounts of sins accumulated in his or her life.

As an example, since Satan has accumulated the most sins in his life, he will burn the longest on planet earth before his spirit body is burned into ashes. In fact because Satan has accumulated the most sins in his life, as he burns in the lake of fire (Revelation 20:10), he will see all of the wicked burn to ashes before his own eternal demise takes place.

After the lake of fire, called "everlasting fire" (See Jude 7, as an example.), which envelopes the earth and the vicinity of space, burns all of the impurities of sin and sinner into ashes, the fire will have nothing else to burn; therefore the "everlasting fire" will eventually go out. When that happens, the elements of the earth and the elements in the vicinity of the earth will be purified from all of the contaminants, and from all sins and sinners. Sin and sinner will be no more. Christ will have a clean universe after all.

After the earth and its vicinity are purified by fire, God will create a new earth and a new heaven in order to accommodate the redeemed, New Jerusalem, the tree of life, the throne of God the Father, God the Christ, and of the redeemed. (Revelation 3:21.)

Regarding the new heavens, new earth, and New Jerusalem, here is the following description by the prophet of the LORD of hosts:

"1 AND I saw a new heaven and a new earth for the first heaven and the first earth were passed away; and there was no more sea. 2 A I John saw the holy city, new Jerusalem, coming down from God out of heaven prepared as a bride adorned for her husband. 3 And I heard a great voice out of heaven saying, Behold, the tabernacle of God is with men, and He will dwell with them, and they shall be His people, and God Himself shall be with them, and he be their God. 4 And God shall wipe away all tears from their eyes; and there shall be no more death, neither sorrow, nor crying neither shall there be any more pain: for the former things are passed away. 5 And He that sat upon the throne said, Behold, I make all things new. And He said unto me, Write: for these words are true and faithful. 6 And He said unto me, It is done, I am Alpha and Omega, the beginning and the end. I will give unto him that is athirst of the fountain of water of life freely. 7 He that overcometh shall inherit all things; and I will be His God, and he shall be My son. 8 But the fearful and the unbelieving, and the abominable, and murderers, and whoremongers, and sorcerers, and idolaters, and all liars, shall have their part in the lake which burneth with fire and brimstone: which is the second death." Revelation 21:1-8

*Ghosts Demons UFO'S and Dead Men*     By: Philip Mitanidis
**Dead Men are They Really Dead**

As per the above verses, the second death, therefore, for the majority of all the evil men and women, would be their second death. Once when they died before the seventh plague of Revelation chapter sixteen ends, and then, their second death will take place after they are resurrected at the end of the one thousand years. Their second death will be caused by the raging fire, at the end of the one thousand years.

For some people, the second death will take place during their third death. Their first death takes place before Christ comes the second time. Their second death will take place for them after the special resurrection takes place (Rev. 1:7), which is during Christ second coming. And their third death will take place when they are resurrected at the end of the one thousand years. At that time, the fires of purification will lap up and consume all of the wicked into "ashes" and "be no more."

But the first death for Satan and his evil angels, will take place during the second death of all the wicked men and women. Their death, along with all of the wicked men and women, will take place during the inferno of the lake of fire that will take place at the end of the one thousand years.

After the fire completes its purification, Christ's universe will, once again, be restored to its original sinless perfect state that it was before the unrepentant sinners decided to destroy it and themselves.

Therefore, since sin and sinner will "be no more," as the above short presentation states, there is not going to be a place of torment forever and ever somewhere in

God's universe because, as the prophet of the LORD has stated before, according to the inspired Scripture (Bible), sin and sinner will be burned into "ashes." They will be no more! And that being the case, the saved from planet earth and the rest of the beings throughout the universe, who have not sinned, will not view the wicked beings tormented or burn endlessly, throughout eternity, in Christ's universe because they will "be no more."

As it was stated before, it should be remembered, as per the inspired Scriptures (Bible), the wicked men, women, Satan, and his evil angels, will be consumed by fire because they do not posses immortality. We are told only God has immortality (1 Timothy 6:13-16).

Therefore, since the wicked men, women, Satan, and his evil angels do not possess immortality, they are going to "be no more." Consequently, it cannot be said, as it is said so often, today, by the majority that there is a place called "hell" where all of the wicked are tormented forever and ever.

Le me say again, if the wicked are immortal they cannot burn and be tormented in "hell-fire" forever and ever. But because they are all mortal beings, the inferno of global fire will burn them up into "ashes."

Christ the LORD of hosts confirms the above comments; He says:

> "[1] behold, the day cometh, that shall burn as an oven; and all the proud, yea, and all that do wickedly, shall be stubble: and the day that cometh shall burn them up, saith the LORD of host, that it

shall leave them neither root nor branch.

"₃ And ye shall tread down the wicked; for they shall be ashes under the soles of your feet in the day that I shall do this, saith the LORD of hosts" (Malachi 4:1, 3).

So, for anyone to say that the wicked men and women will be tormented in "brimstone and hell-fire" for ever and ever is incorrect because according to the above verses, all of the wicked will burn into "ashes." They will become ashes because they do not possess immortality.

By the way, for anyone to say, and as it is said that only wicked men and women will be tormented forever and ever in hell and not Satan and his evil angels, is placing Satan and his evil angels into exclusion. Why would anyone say that only wicked men and women are going to be tormented in hell, and not Satan and his angels, is a good question? Don't you think since Satan and his evil angels deceived, tormented, tempted, mislead men and women from receiving eternal salvation, and caused all of the men and women to continuously sin that Satan and his evil angels should be the ones tormented in hell-fire instead of the wicked men and women?

So! Why are immortality believers so quick to condemn the wicked men and women of planet earth into eternal inferno instead of Satan and his evil angels? Haven't they heard the words of Christ the LORD that hell-fire is also reserved for Satan and his evil angels? (See Ezekiel 28:16, 19; Matthew 25:41; Revelation 20:10.)

But irrespective what doctrine of immortality

people believe in, or prefer to believe in, it cannot be true because 1), we are told by the inspired Scriptures (Bible) that "only God has immortality" (1 Timothy 6:16). 2), men, women, children, Satan, and his evil angels do not have or possess immortality (Job 4:17; 1 Corinthians 15: 53); and 3), all of the wicked men, women, Satan, and his evil angels will be consumed by "everlasting fire" until they all turn into "ashes" (Malachi 4:1, 3). The LORD said to Satan, "$_{16}$ I will destroy thee [you], O covering cherub, from the midst of the stones of fire" and "$_{19}$ never shalt thou [you] be any more" (Ezekiel 28:16, 19).

So, how can anyone insist, contrary to the above Biblical statements that today, the wicked dead are immortal and burning in hell-fire somewhere in Christ's universe?

In summary: Man is "mortal" (Job 4:17). And because he is "mortal," he "seeks immortality" (Romans 2:6, 7). The righteous "seek immortality" from God because "only" God has "immortality" (1 Timothy 6:13-16). And because man does not have immortality, evil men and women will be consumed by fire until they are turned into "ashes" (Malachi 4:1, 3).

Let me say again: If evil men, women, Satan, and his evil angels had or possessed immortality, the fire would not be able to consume them, hurt them, torture them, or turn them into "ashes." But because they do not possess immortality, Christ says that they with Satan and his evil angels will be consumed by fire and "be no more." And that extinction, by fire, of evil men, women, Satan, and evil angels is called the "second death"

(Revelation 20:14).

And the fact that there is a "second death," for evil men and women that alone should suffice in dispersing the idea that evil dead men and women are alive and gone to hell to be tormented for ever and ever.

Therefore, presently, all dead men and women are really dead waiting in their graves for their respective resurrections; "29 they that have done good, unto the resurrection of life [where they will all receive immortality]; and they that have done evil, unto the resurrection of damnation [where they will all receive annihilation by fire]" (John 5:29).

"48 What man is he that liveth, and shall not see death? shall he deliver his soul from the hand of the grave?" (Psalms 89:48).

# **CONSIDERING FEW OBJECTIONS**

Although the prophets of the LORD, in the previous pages, have clearly stated that man does not possess immortality, many individuals misquote a number of Bible verses to support their immortality soul or spirit doctrine. In doing so, they posture these verses against Christ the LORD of host when He says that He will bring the wicked into "ashes" (Malachi 4:1, 3), and further posture their pet verses against the verses, which clearly state that "only God has immortality" (1 Timothy 6:13-16).

If you are not familiar with the misquoted verses, which are brought forward to support the immortality of man, I will bring few more verses, for your consideration, so that you can observe the inappropriate use of the immortal soul doctrine.

## **Absent from the Body**

You would think verses like 1 Timothy 6:13-16 should suffice to disregard the immortal soul doctrine, as being a Biblical truth; but because people prefer to cling to their immortal soul beliefs they bring other Scripture references, which have no referral to or connection with an immortal soul doctrine as proof that man has an immortal soul.

In order to support the theory that man is immortal and that he has an immortal soul, such are the following verses coined in 2 Corinthians 5:1-9 by the immortal soul believers.

**Absent from the Body**

The immortal soul believer says that it is evident from Paul's statement in 2 Corinthians 5:6, 8 that the righteous dead go to heaven immediately at death; therefore man possesses an immortal soul.

But what the immortal soul believers fail to mention is the fact that in 2 Corinthians 5:1-9, Apostle Paul is strictly talking about his earthly body and not about having an immortal spirit or soul. And notably, Apostle Paul does not reveal, in this presentation, when the transition will take place between his mortal human body and the immortal heavenly body, the duration it takes to receive the immortal body, and when will the immortal body be given to him so that he could be with Christ the LORD.

Like 2 Corinthians 5:1-9, some verses are not fully explained. As examples, consider the following five excerpts and notice how Christ and the prophets do not give us all of the information regarding the subject matter, which they present to us.

1). In this brief presentation, Apostle Paul is "betwixt two" decisions, he says, "22 But if I live in the flesh, this is the fruit of my labour: yet what I shall choose I wot not. 23 For I am in a strait betwixt two, having a desire to depart, and to be with Christ; which is far better" (Philippians 1:22, 23).

2). In another place he says, "1 IT is not expedient for me doubtless to glory. I will come to visions and revelations of the LORD. 2 I knew a man in Christ above fourteen years ago, (whether in the body, I cannot tell; or whether out of the body, I cannot tell; God knoweth:) such an one caught up to the third heaven. 3 And I knew such a man, (whether in the body, or out of the body, I cannot tell: God knoweth:) 4 How that he was caught up into paradise, and heard unspeakable words, which it is not lawful for a man to utter" (2 Corinthians 12:1-4).

3). In this narrative, Isaiah wrote, "1 THE Spirit of the Lord GOD is upon Me: because the LORD hath anointed Me to preach good tidings unto the meek; he hath sent Me to bind up the brokenhearted, to proclaim liberty to the captives, and the opening of the prison to them that are bound; 2 To proclaim the acceptable year of the LORD, and the day of vengeance of our God; to comfort all that mourn" (Isaiah 61:1, 2).

And, in reference to Isaiah's passage, Christ the LORD of hosts read, "18 The Spirit of the Lord is upon Me: because he hath anointed Me to preach the gospel to the poor; he hath sent Me to heal the brokenhearted, to preach deliverance to the captives, and recovering of sight to the blind, to set at liberty them that are bruised, 19 To preach the acceptable year of the Lord." Luke 4:18, 19

Compare the omission of the words, "and the day of vengeance of our God;" by Jesus Christ; they are not explained in Luke 4:18, 19. We are not told when the "vengeance of our God" will take place?

4). In another incident, Christ the LORD of hosts will say, at His second coming, to the wicked men, women, Satan, and to Satan's evil angels "depart into everlasting fire." But, as you will notice, Christ the LORD of hosts does not explain when they are going to be plunged into the everlasting fire.

Here is His statement:

> "41 Then shall He say unto them on the left hand, Depart from Me, ye [all of you] cursed, unto everlasting fire, prepared for the devil and his angels" (Matthew 25:41).

5). Again, in the following verses, you will find that the day of the Lord is not explained or when the elements of the earth will "melt with fervent heat"?

> "10 in the which the heavens shall pass away with a great noise, and the elements shall melt with fervent heat, the earth also and the works that are therein shall be burned up. 11 Seeing then that all these things shall be dissolved, what manner of persons ought ye to be in all holy conversation and godliness, 12 Looking for and hasting unto the coming of the day of God, wherein the heavens being on fire shall be dissolved, and the elements shall melt with fervent heat?" 2 Peter 3:10-12

As you can readily see from the above verses, Apostle Peter, like Isaiah, Jesus Christ the LORD of hosts, and Apostle Paul, does not explain to us in his presentation when the fires of inferno are going to "melt the elements" of planet earth and its surroundings?

And so it is with Apostle Paul, he does not expand in the following presentation what takes place from the time he desires to be "clothed" with a heavenly body and up until the time he actually receives his heavily immortal body so that he can be with Jesus Chris the LORD.

> The verses read as follows: "1 FOR we know that if our earthly house of this tabernacle were dissolved, we have a building of God, an house not made with hands, eternal in the heavens. 2 For in this we groan, earnestly desiring to be clothed upon with our house which is from heaven: 3 If so be that being clothed we shall not be found naked. 4 For we that are in this tabernacle do groan, being burdened: not for that we would be unclothed, but clothed upon, that mortality might be swallowed up of life. 5 Now he that hath wrought us for the selfsame thing is God, who also hath given unto us the earnest of the Spirit. 6 Therefore we are always confident, knowing that, whilst we are at home in the body, we are absent from the LORD: 7 (For we walk by faith, not by sight. 8 We are confident, I say, and willing rather to be absent from the body, and to be present with the LORD. 9 Wherefore we labour, that, whether present or absent, we may be accepted of Him." 2 Corinthians 5:1-9

As you have read, there is no explanation provided regarding the duration from the time when the mortal body is "dissolved" to the putting on an "immortal" body.

In fact, Paul does not tell us in the above verses when the immortal body is received?

Nonetheless, there are at least five predominant points that are brought to our attention in his presentation.

<u>One,</u> the "earthly house" is the carnal human body.

<u>Two,</u> the carnal human body can be "dissolved."

<u>Three,</u> the human body is mortal "earthly."

<u>Four,</u> in none of the nine verses do we find mentioned one single word about an immortal soul going to be with the LORD at death! Apostle Paul, in all of the nine verses, does not speak about a soul or a spirit departing from the body. He concentrates and strictly speaks about what happens to the human body and his preference "to be clothed upon" with an immortal body so that he can be with the LORD, which he prefers.

<u>Five,</u> in this presentation, as you have read, there is a gap between the time Paul wants to be with the LORD and the actual occurrence when he would be with the LORD; that time period is not discussed in the nine verses. Apostle Paul does not reveal when the righteous human mortal body is going to receive immortality; he clarifies that point in his other presentations.

But, for one thing, although the apostle does not mention, in this presentation, when our "earthly house" is going to "dissolved," we are told in verse one that "our earthly house" (body) does "dissolve." And, we are also assured in verse one that "if our earthly house [body] were dissolved," we have an "eternal" "house" (body) that is going to be given to the righteous.

Then, in verse two, Apostle Paul explains why the righteous desire "to be clothed" with their "house [body] which is from heaven." The answer is given; so that "we shall not be found naked" (v.3). And the reason Apostle Paul wants us to be "clothed" with our heavenly "house" (body) is to have our mortal "earthly" (body) "swallowed up of life" (v.4). And if our mortal body is "swallowed," it means that we are going to be saved in Christ's kingdom. But, if our earthly house (body) is not "swallowed," we are going to be "naked." And if we are found "naked," it means that we are not going to be saved in Christ's kingdom. Therefore Apostle Paul prefers to be "clothed." And if he is "clothed," he knows that he is going to receive an immortal "heavenly body" and be with Christ. And as he says, "8 not to me only, but unto all them also that love His appearing" (2 Timothy 4:8).

And, starting from verse six, Apostle Paul further explains; he says; "whilst we are at home [on earth] in the body, we are absent from the LORD." As long as we are here on planet earth in our earthly mortal body, we are absent from the LORD; and we will remain absent from the LORD if we do not receive an immortal body. On the other hand, Apostle Paul says that we are "confident"

**Absent from the Body**

and "willing rather to be absent from the body, and to be present with the LORD." And, in order, to be present with the LORD, a person has to first put on the heavenly immortal body (v.8).

But, the question is, when is that immortal heavenly body going to be received so that Apostle Paul would be with the LORD—that portions is not explained in his presentation. He only says that he is "willing" to be "absent" from his earthly body and "clothed" with a heavenly body so that he can be "present with the LORD." But, in order to be accepted by Christ the LORD of hosts, Apostle Paul says that he "labours" towards that goal.

To clarify the verse it will read as follows: "8 We are confident, I say, and willing rather to be absent from the body [earthly body], and to be present with the LORD [in his immortal body]. 9 Wherefore we labour, that, whether present or absent, we may be accepted of Him." 2 Corinthians 5:8, 9

Therefore, as you can see from the above verses, Apostle Paul does not mention anywhere that man has an immortal soul or an immortal spirit. He strictly talks about a mortal body and putting on an immortal body. But nowhere does he state in the above verses when his immortal body is going to be given to him so that he could be with Christ the LORD of hosts.

Nonetheless, since the apostle does not tell us, in verses one to nine, when his righteous body is going to be "redeemed" (Romans 8:23), or when the righteous dead or living are going to put on their immortal heavenly bodies, we have to go to few other references where he explains to us when mortality is swallowed up and when are the immortal bodies going to be given to the righteous (redeemed).

Here is one of those references.

In first Thessalonians chapter four, Apostle Paul speaks about the second coming of Christ the LORD of hosts and of the resurrection of the righteous. He says;

> "13 But I would not have you to be ignorant, brethren, concerning them which are asleep [dead], that ye sorrow not, even as others which have no hope. 14 For if we believe that Jesus died and rose again, even so them also which sleep in Jesus will God bring with Him. 15 For this we say unto you by the word of the LORD, that we which are alive and remain unto the coming of the LORD shall not prevent [precede] them which are asleep [dead].

> "16 For the LORD Himself shall descend from heaven with a shout, with the voice of the archangel, and with the trump of God: and the dead in Christ shall rise first: 17 Then we which are alive and remain shall be caught up together with them in the air: so shall we ever be with the LORD. 18 Wherefore comfort one another with these words." 1 Thessalonians 4:13-18

In verse sixteen, Apostle Paul says the following:

> "¹⁶ For the LORD Himself shall descend from heaven with a shout, with the voice of the archangel, and with the trump of God: and the dead in Christ shall rise first" (1 Thessalonians 4:16).

Did you notice?

Paul states, "the dead in Christ shall rise first."

When will the "dead in Christ rise first"?

According to the above verse, the "dead in Christ shall rise first" at Christ's second coming.

Who are the dead that will rise "first"?

According to first Thessalonians chapter four and verse fourteen, they are the righteous who "sleep [are dead] in Christ."

If you recall, previously, we discussed that the righteous dead in Christ will be resurrected first (John 5:28, 29). At that time, it was stated why the righteous would be resurrected first. It was because the unrighteous (unsaved) will remain in their deathbeds until the "second resurrection," which takes place at the end of the one thousand years. The second resurrection is the first resurrection for the majority of the wicked (Rev. 20:5)

Therefore, the "first" resurrection for the righteous takes place, as 1 Thessalonians 4:16 states, at the second coming of Christ the LORD of hosts. And the first resurrection for the majority of the ungodly takes place after the one thousand years expire (Revelation 20:5).

Consequently, as 1 Thessalonians chapter four and

verse sixteen states, at the second coming of Christ the LORD of hosts, the righteous will "rise" and will be given immortal bodies. Apostle Paul adds,

> "20 we look for the Saviour, the LORD Jesus Christ; 21 Who shall change our vile body, that it may be fashioned like unto His glorious body, according to the working whereby He is able even to subdue all things unto Himself" (Philippians 3:20, 21).

How quickly will the righteous "mortal" earthly bodies (houses) be changes into "immortal" bodies (houses)?

Apostle Paul explains;

> "51 Behold, I shew you a mystery; We shall not all sleep [be dead], but we shall all be changed. 52 In a moment, in the twinkling of an eye, at the last trump: for the trumpet shall sound [1 Thess. 4:16], and the dead shall be raised incorruptible, and we shall be changed. 53 For this corruptible must put on incorruption, and this mortal must put on immortality. 54 So when this corruptible shall have put on incorruption, and this mortal shall have put on immortality, then shall be brought to pass the saying that is written [Hosea 13:14], Death is swallowed up in victory" (1 Corinthians 15:51-54)."

So! According to the above verses, when do the

## Absent from the Body

righteous put on their immortal "heavenly house" (body)?

They put on their "immortal" heavenly houses (bodies) when Christ the LORD of hosts, at His second coming (at the "last trump"), calls His people, dead and alive, to Himself "(1 Thessalonians 4:16, 17).

> "$_{16}$ For the LORD Himself shall descend from heaven with a shout, with the voice of the archangel, and with the trump of God: and the dead in Christ shall rise first. $_{17}$ Then we which are alive and remain [Hebrews 11:39, 40] shall be caught up together with them in the clouds [angels], to meet the LORD in the air: and so shall we ever be with the LORD" (1 Thessalonians 4:16, 17).

Since Christ the LORD of hosts and Apostle Paul, refer to death of a person as "sleep," you can readily understand why Paul emulates the duration of death as being a "moment" in time. He does because when a person dies his earthly body turns into dust and his thoughts "perish" (Psalm 146:4; 115:17). And since a person, at death, cannot praise the LORD or think, it means that, at death, there is no consciousness. And since there is no consciousness at death, when he or she is resurrected, the duration of death becomes like a moment in time.

The psalmist reminds us by saying that at death a person's "$_4$ breath goeth forth, he returneth to his earth; in that very day his thoughts perish" (Psalms 146:4).

And then, he adds,

> "₁₇ The dead praise not the LORD, neither any that go down into silence [grave]" (Psalms 115:17).

Therefore, when Apostle Paul makes the statement that he prefers to be with Christ the LORD, it is obvious, he and likeminded people, prefer to be with Christ the LORD; but they cannot be with Him right now because like King David and Apostle Paul they have not received their heavenly houses (bodies). (See Acts 2:29, 34; John 3:13; Revelation 20:13, 14.) They, like the rest of the righteous dead and righteous living are still waiting for Christ the LORD of hosts to come and give them their immortal "heavenly houses" (bodies). Apostle Paul says, "₈ not to me only; but unto all them also that love His appearing" (2 Timothy 4:8). (See Philippians 3:20, 21.)

But until then, Apostle Paul concludes by saying, "Wherefore we labour, that, whether present or absent, we may be accepted of Him" (2 Corinthians 5:9).

Thus, until the second coming of Christ the LORD of hosts (John 14:3), Apostle Paul admonishes us "₁₈ to comfort one another with these words [1 Thessalonians 4:13-17]" (1 Thessalonians 4:18).

## The Transfiguration

In support to the immortal soul doctrine, the immortal soul believers say, "When Christ the LORD of hosts was transfigured, on the mount, 'Moses and Elias talking with Him.' The fact that Moses was there, it definitely proves that man is an immortal soul because Moses, if you recall, had died on mount Nebo and was buried by Christ the LORD of hosts just before the children of Israel crossed the River Jordan."

The record states: "1 AND after six days Jesus taketh Peter, James, and John his brother, and bringeth them up into an high mountain apart, 2 And was transfigured before them: and His face did shine as the sun, and His raiment was white as the light; 3 And behold, there appeared unto them Moses and Elias [Elijah] talking with Him. 4 Then answered Peter, and said unto Jesus, LORD, it is good for us to be here: if thou wilt, let us make here three tabernacles; one for Thee, and one for Moses, and one for Elias [Elijah]. 5 While He yet spake, behold, a bright cloud overshadowed them: and behold a voice out of the cloud, which said, This is my beloved Son, in whom I am well pleased; hear ye Him. 6 And when the disciples heard it, they fell on their face, and were sore afraid. 7 And Jesus came and touched them, and said, Arise, and be not afraid. 8 And when they had lifted up their eyes, they saw no man, save Jesus only. 9 And as they came down from the mountain, Jesus charged them, saying, Tell the vision to no man, until the Son of man be risen again from the dead" (Matthew 17:1-9).

There are two ways to view this transfiguration

incident: as a vision or as a literal event.

If we view the transfiguration as a vision, then the claim that Moses is or was an immortal soul who appeared on the mount of transfiguration is pointless because in visions the presentation to a prophet could have pictures in his mind of animals, birds, fish, men, and events without either of the animals, bids, fish, men, or the events being literal at that moment and actually before him. (See Daniel 7:1-8; 8:1-12, as examples.)

But, if we view the incident as literal, then the claim that Moses was or is a immortal soul is equally pointless, for the transfiguration narrative says nothing about an immaterial spirit, or soul, called Moses, hovering beside Christ the LORD of hosts. Instead we read that Christ was present, and beside Him, "Moses and Elias [Elijah]" was present. We know that Elias [Elijah] was translated bodily to heaven (2 Kings 2:11); therefore, we can say that Elias [Elijah] was also real. And there is nothing in the account to suggest that Moses was any less real. The account does not say that Moses' spirit or Moses' soul was there; instead, it says that Moses was there beside Christ the LORD.

Furthermore, as you have read, there is nothing in the above presentation, which reveals that Moses and Elias possess immortality.

What the transfiguration record does is to reveal the two righteous classes of people that are going to appear before Christ the LORD of hosts when He comes the second time to take His saints home. They are the righteous dead who are going to be resurrected, as Moses was (Jude 9), and the righteous living who are going to be translated, as Elias [Elijah] was (2 Kings 2:11).

Therefore, the transfiguration provides support, not for the immortal soul doctrine, freed from the shell of a body, but for the doctrine of the resurrection of the righteous dead and of the transformation of the righteous living, at the second coming of Christ the LORD of hosts.

## **Lazarus and the Rich Man.**

The verses in this parable read as follows:

"19 There was a certain rich man, which was clothed in purple and fine linen, and fared sumptuously every day; 20 And there was a certain beggar named Lazarus, which was laid at his gate full of sores, 21 And desiring to be fed with the crumbs which fell from the rich man's table: moreover the dogs came and licked his sores. 22 And it came to pass, that the beggar died, and was carried by the angels into Abraham's bosom: the rich man also died, and was buried; 23 And in hell he lift up his eyes, being in torments, and seeth Abraham afar off, and Lazarus in his bosom. 24 And he cried and said, Father Abraham, have mercy on me and send Lazarus, that he may dip the tip of his finger in water, and cool my tongue; for I am tormented in this flame. 25 But Abraham said, Son, remember that thou in thy lifetime receivedst thy good things, and likewise Lazarus evil things: but now he is comforted, and thou art tormented. 26 And beside all this, between us and you there is a great gulf fixed: so that they which would pass from hence to you cannot; neither can they pass to us, that would come from thence. 27 Then he said, I pray thee therefore, father, that thou wouldest send him to my father's house: 28 For I have five brethren; that he may testify unto them, lest they also come into this place of torment. 29 Abraham saith unto him, They have Moses and the prophets; let them hear them. 30 And he said, Nay, father Abraham; but if one went unto them from the dead, they will repent. 31 And he said unto him, If they hear not Moses and the prophets, neither will they be persuaded, though one rose from the dead." Luke 16:19-31

If you believe in the immortal soul doctrine and use the above presentation to prove your stance, here are couple of points to consider.

If we view the parable of "the rich man" and "Lazarus," as a vision, the argument for immortality becomes pointless because in visions, as you well know, a prophet can be presented with dogs, men, children, women, trees, animals, mountains, planets, stars, etc., etc., without these things being tangible.

But, if we view Lazarus and the rich man literally, and claim that Lazarus and the rich man are immortal, it is equally pointless because men, women, and children do not go to heaven, at death, in the flesh, which immortal soul believers agree; and because they further agree that heaven does not exist in Abraham's bosom where God, the holy angels, and the redeemed live in. As it was stated earlier, no men, women, or children go to heaven at death, in the flesh, which the immortal soul believers also agree. And since they agree that the three bodies and the body parts of verses twenty-two, twenty-three, and twenty-four refer to literal bodies and body parts— "mouth," "eyes," and "fingers," plus "flame" and "water" are real, this parable cannot be used to prove that people are immortal. But, more importantly because Scripture

## Lazarus and the Rich Man

states that evil man does not possess immortality and neither is he given immortality at death. In fact, eventually unrepentant evil man will be burnt into ashes and be no more. (See Malachi 4:1-3.)

Therefore, we have to conclude, since there is no evidence in the parable, which reveals that Abraham, Lazarus, and the rich man have immortal souls or bodies, and live in heaven and in hell, we have to deduce that the story is an allegory, simile, and a parable. Therefore, I would like to give you two overviews of the parable.

First, if Jesus is not talking about real souls and spirits, what was His point?

The real point of the parable is capsulated in the answer that was given to the rich man by Abraham. The rich man, if you recall, pleaded with Abraham that Lazarus be sent to warn his brothers to avoid making the same horrible mistake as he had made and end up in "torment" (v.28).

Speaking to Abraham, the rich man said, "27 I pray thee therefore, father, that thou wouldest send him to my father's house: 28 For I have five brethren; that he may testify unto them, lest they also come into this place of torment" (Luke 16:27, 28).

In response, Abraham wanted to direct the rich man away from him by saying to the rich man, "29 They have Moses and the prophets; let them hear them" (Luke 16:29). That is the main point Christ was making to His tempters. Did you notice? Christ said, "They" the Jews, "have Moses and the prophets; let them hear them."

But, Christ did not stop there; He continued to

enforce His point by saying, "31 if they hear not Moses and the prophets, neither will they be persuaded, though one rose from the dead" (Luke 16:31.

As you know, Christ did resurrect many individuals from their death, during His three and a half years of ministry; did the Jews (Judah) and his five brothers (tribes) listen to them? In fact, Christ resurrected His friend Lazarus from his grave (John 11:34-47); did they listen to him? As per Scripture, some did, but the majority, obviously they did not!

And, if "one rose from the dead" today, would they or you believe that person's report that "the dead know not anything" (Ecclesiastes 9:5); and at death, their "thoughts perish" (Psalms 146:4); and because the inspired word of God the Holy Spirit plainly states, "the soul that sinneth, it shall die" (Ezekiel 18:4)?

So! Since the soul of a person dies at death, how can Abraham, Lazarus, and the rich man be immortal and alive in their respective environments?

They are not immortal because, as we have studied before, only God has immortality. (See 1 Timothy 6:13-16.) None of the created beings possess immortality.

Therefore, the main point Jesus Christ the LORD of hosts was making to the Sadducees, Pharisees, priests, and to all of the Jews who placed their faith in Abraham, for their salvation, was the fact that the Jews (Judah), mainly the Jewish leaders, were rejecting Christ as the Messiah, as their LORD God and Savior, His claims, and His ministry because like many people of today, they would not take the time to verify what Moses had written

## Lazarus and the Rich Man

about Jesus Christ the LORD of hosts.

Many of the Jews, especially the Jewish leaders because they believed that Christ was born in Galilee, they argued with the people, in order to disqualify Christ's claims, they said that the real Messiah would not be born in Galilee—as if Jesus was. Therefore, some believed that "41 This is the Christ. But some said, Shall Christ come out of Galilee? 42 Hath not the scripture said, That Christ cometh of the seed of David, and out of the town of Bethlehem [Micah 5:2], where David was? 43 So there was a division among the people because of Him" (John 7:41-43).

Thus, the Jewish leaders, and those who followed their deceptive advice, treated Jesus Christ as an imposture, delusional, and as a mere man. They said, "3 Is not this the carpenter, the son of Mary, the brother of James, and Joses, and Judah, and Simon? and are not His sisters here with us? And they were offended of Him" (Mark 6:3).

In fact, they even ridiculed Him all the way to the cross. At the cross, "35 the people stood beholding, Him, saying, He saved others; let Him save Himself, if He be Christ, the chosen of God. 36 And the soldiers also mocked Him, coming to Him, and offering Him vinegar. 37 And saying, If Thou be the king of Jews, save Thyself" (Luke 23:35-37).

Christ could not save Himself. He was on a mission. He came in the flesh to die for the penitent sinners of planet earth. And that is what He did. He came and accomplished His mission and fulfilled the "promise" He made to Adam; and that is, through

Christ's sacrifice, Adam and his offspring would be saved from their eternal demise, if they wanted to.

But now, since He came, as He had promised, to His own people who are called by His name, they rejected Him by arguing, if He could not save Himself, how was he going to save us from the grave? Therefore, the Jews wrote-off Christ as an impostor and taught their children to do the same.

Thus, Jesus Christ the LORD of hosts spoke in a parable to confront the callous attitude that was propagated towards Him by the majority of the Jewish leaders. They refused to accept Christ's testimony that He was the LORD God and Savior of their forefathers. Instead, they clung to their belief that they had Abraham their father. So! Why did they need Christ the impostor to sway them to believe otherwise?

They did need Him because without Christ the LORD there is no salvation. Christ stated that fact many, many times in the Old Testament. From Mount Sinai, Christ the LORD of hosts said, "$_2$ I am the LORD thy [Your] God, which have brought thee out of the land of Egypt, out of the house of bondage. $_3$ Thou shalt have no other gods before Me" (Exodus 20:2, 3). And through the pen of Hosea, Christ the LORD of hosts said, "$_4$ I am the LORD thy God from the land of Egypt, and thou [you] shalt know no god but Me: for there is no Saviour beside Me" (Hosea 13:4).

Although it was widely accepted by the children of Israel that salvation was granted to them by the God of Abraham, the Jews (Judah) rejected the salvation of the

God of Abraham when He came to them in the flesh, as He had promised, in order to offer Himself a sacrifice for the penitent sinners (John 1:29). Without Christ's supreme sacrifice on Calvary's cross, there would be no salvation for anyone. We are told, "12 Neither is there salvation in any other: for there is none other name under heaven given among men, whereby we might be saved" (Acts 4:12). And Christ the LORD of hosts added by the pen of Isaiah saying, "11 I am the LORD; and beside Me there is no Saviour" (Isaiah 43:11).

    The Levi priests knew this to be a fact because the sin offering that was brought by the sinner, pointed forward to the coming of the God of Abraham in the flesh, in order to pay for the sins of the penitent sinners. Every day the Levi priests had to take the sinner's animal, place it on the altar of sacrifice, burn it, and then, go into the "holy place" of the Sanctuary—first room—and offer, according to Moses, their prayers to Christ the LORD of hosts, by standing before the "table of incense." The sin offering and thank offering took place twice a day, in the morning and before dusk, in the eastern courtyard of the Sanctuary.

    But, when Christ offered Himself on Calvary's cross, as an atoning sacrifice for the penitent sinners, why did the Levite priests continued with the animal burnt offerings for the sinner's sins? They knew that the animals could not and would not take away the sins of the sinner? (See Hebrews 10:1-4)

    So! Since Moses and the rest of the prophets reveal that Christ the LORD of hosts is the God of Abraham and the Savior, why was Judah (Jews) rejecting Christ (Messiah) and His sacrifice?

They did because they would not consult Moses and the rest of the prophets in order to confirm Christ's claims that He was the One the prophets were looking forward to His coming, in the flesh, as He had "promised." (See 1 Peter 1:9-12.) By not consulting Scripture, the Jews clung to their belief that they were going to be saved no matter what because they were the chosen people of the God of Abraham.

Therefore because the Jews continued to reject Christ the LORD of hosts, He exposed their callous hearts, the rejection of Him as their LORD God and Savior, and foretold of the outcome of the rich man and Lazarus by bringing five familiar individualities to their attention in the form of a parable. They are: "the rich man," "Lazarus," "Abraham," "Moses," and Jesus Christ the King of Israel (2 Samuel 7:26; Matthew 21:5). And in addition to the above witnesses, Christ included the five brothers of the rich man (Judah). These individuals had their own distinct personalities.

The rich man, in Christ's parable, who was dressed in "purple" and "fine linen" represents Judah or Jews, if you like, and the Levitical priesthood. ("Purple" represents Judah. "Fine linen" represents the Levitical priesthood.) But mainly, the clothing of the rich man represents the upper echelon of the Jewish system; and that is, the elders, priests, Sadducees, and the Pharisees. And that does not exclude those who held office in the Sanhedrin. It represents more precisely the leaders of

## Lazarus and the Rich Man

Judah because they were the teachers, lawyers, priests, elders, and policy makers. Unfortunately, these leaders of Judah made their followers to adhere to their voice and not to the voice of the LORD or to His prophets that were sent to them; in fact they killed them (Matthew 23:37). Instead of believing Moses and the prophets, they continued to listen to their leader's misrepresentation of the words of the prophets, and therefore became steeped in their traditions (Matthew 15:1-9) instead of the Torah.

Being steeped in their tradition, it meant that Judah had already fallen into apostasy. If Judah, during Christ's time, had not fallen into apostasy, the Jewish leaders would have adhered to the prophecies that were spoken by the prophets of old; therefore they would have accepted Jesus Christ the LORD of hosts as the Messiah, and as their LORD God and Savior. In doing so, they would have continued to represent Christ the LORD of hosts to the world, as did their forefathers, and the prophets of old. They would have preached that Christ is the Messiah (John 4:25, 26; Mark 14:61, 62). They would have preached of His supreme sacrifice for the repentant sinners. They would have preached of His resurrection. And, they would have continued to preach to the world, today, the Gospel of Jesus Christ the LORD of hosts (Mark 1:1) bringing peace of mind and hope to sinners everywhere of eternal life, happiness, and contentment that is found in the Kingdom of Christ the LORD of hosts. But, since Judah (Jews) refused to accept Christ's coming in the flesh, His atoning sacrifice on Calvary's cross, and refused to preach the Gospel of Jesus Christ, as

Abraham did, Christ would choose the Gentiles to preach His Gospel to the world. In doing so, the privileges, which Judah (Jews) had, they were going to be taken away from them and given to the Gentiles. And to make that point convincing, Jesus Christ used Lazarus to represent the Gentiles.

According to Christ's parable, Lazarus did not belong to the Jewish club of exclusion. He, like many of the Gentiles, was an individual who was seated at the gates of Jerusalem, called a sinner, an outcast, a beggar, a dog, a scavenger, a parasite, and much more. But, all was not lost, by sitting at the gates of Jerusalem. Lazarus received some truths from the passersby—"bread crumbs"—indirectly from the Torah about the God of Abraham. And that hurt Lazarus very much because he, like many Gentiles, was not allowed to join the exclusive Jewish club or worship with them. Even worse, he was not allowed to bring a sin offering for his sins to Christ the LORD of hosts, and place it on the altar of sacrifice, in the eastern courtyard of the sanctuary. He was an outsider looking with his mind's eye, into the "most holy place" of the Sanctuary. He understood, as rumors had it that Christ the LORD of hosts was believed to dwell in between the two cherubims, and contemplated of Christ's love and of His promises. But outside of his thoughts, he felt as a reject. In his humiliating painful state, and without hope; the only consolation Lazarus had was from his Gentile friends (dogs). The "dogs" had more sympathy upon Lazarus than the Jews (rich man).

Although the Jews (Judah), according to Moses,

## Lazarus and the Rich Man

were to listen to what Christ had to say and pass on the teachings of the Torah to the Gentiles (See Acts 7:37, 38.), they refused and are still refusing the counsel of Moses, as the parable indicates.

Abraham was and still is the father figure of the Jewish believer. The Jews were comfortable in believing that they were the descendants of Abraham and the chosen people. And because of that ideology, they believed that they would always be saved and the Gentiles lost.

Unfortunately for them, as the parable indicates, that philosophy is not true; all you have to do is to read the books of Moses, the book of the Judges, the books of war, and the other prophets to see how the children of Israel fell into apostasy over and over again; in doing so, many lost their eternal life because they had chosen to serve the gods of the heathen.

In the Torah (the five books of Moses), Moses repeatedly refers to Christ the LORD of hosts, starting from Genesis 1:1 and all the way to Deuteronomy 34:12. In fact, we can even include the book of Job where Moses refers to Christ the LORD repeatedly throughout the pages of that book. That is why Jesus was directing the Jews, via Abraham, to consult the writings of Moses.

In fact, Jesus Christ the LORD of hosts tried for three and a half years to convince the Jews that He was the God of their fathers and that Moses wrote about Him (John 5:45-47); but they, like many people of today, did not want to confirm Christ's words by way of Scripture or to listen to the words of Jesus Christ. Because of those facts, Jesus Christ the LORD said to them, "43 Why do ye [all of you] not understand My speech?" And then, Jesus reveals to them the reason why they do not understand what He was saying to them. Jesus said to them, "even because ye [all of you] cannot hear My words" (John 8:43). In other words, they did not take the time to listen to what Christ was saying to them. They ignored Him; and at the end, they rejected Him and crucified Him on Calvary's cross. Apostle John says, "11 He came unto His own, and His own received him not" (John 1:11).

Secondly, having given you a bit of an overview and of the tense conditions that existed in Jerusalem between Jesus Christ the LORD and the Jews, and between the Gentiles and the Jews, here is the additional meaning of the parable of the "rich man" and "Lazarus."

As it was stated before, the personalities in the parable of the rich man and Lazarus are real; people were familiar with them. Therefore, there was no confusion in Christ's presentation of the message He was conveying to the crowd.

Christ the LORD of hosts explains the state of the rich man (Judah) and of Lazarus (Gentiles). Christ said, "19 There was a certain man, which was clothed in purple and fine linen, and fared sumptuously every day: 20 And there was a certain beggar named Lazarus, which was laid at his gate full of sores. 21 And desiring to be fed with the crumbs which fell from the rich man's table; moreover, the dogs came and licked his sores."

By reading the above few verses regarding the rich man and Lazarus, you can readily see that neither of these

## Lazarus and the Rich Man

men are condemned in any way for their life styles by Christ the LORD. As free moral agents, Christ the LORD respected their choice of life styles.

So! Since neither of these men are said to be evildoers, why is Jesus Christ placing the rich man in a setting of hell and not Lazarus?

Should it not be the other way around?

No because Christ the LORD was forecasting to the mixed crowd (Jews and Gentiles) what was going to happen to the rich man (Judah), if Judah did not repent, and what was going to happen to Lazarus (Gentiles) after Christ's crucifixion takes place on Calvary's cross.

According to the parable, Jesus began His revelation to His listeners that the rich man represents the Jewish nation (Judah) by the clothing the rich man was wearing, which distinguished him from the impoverished people around Him. And by the dialogue that was taking place between the rich man and Abraham. Abraham was calling the rich man "Son" (v.25); and the rich man was calling Abraham "father" (vs.24, 30). In other words, the rich man (Jews) claimed to have a personal relationship with Abraham.

In addition, Jesus revealed to the crowd that the rich man (Judah) chose to put his faith in Abraham for his salvation, and how Abraham insisted that the Jews put their trust in the writings of Moses and in the God of Abraham.

By repeatedly rejecting Abraham's counsel, to search the writings of Moses (v.29), regarding Christ the Messiah (John 1:41), the rich man (Judah) finally rejected

Christ the LORD of hosts as his LORD God and Savior (John 1:11); whereby Lazarus (Gentiles) chose to believe in the God of Abraham. (See Acts chapter two.)

And when the rich man and Lazarus died, the rich man was surprised to find himself rejected by Abraham. And even worse, the rich man found himself condemned to "hell"!

Moreover, the rich man was surprised to see Lazarus in the bosom of Abraham. That is, Abraham favored Lazarus because Lazarus took Abraham's advice and went to consult the writings of Moses; and when he found out that Christ is the LORD God of Abraham, Lazarus accepted Jesus Christ as his LORD God and Savior. In doing so, Lazarus received acceptance of Abraham. And because of his acceptance, Lazarus was found comfortably favored and laying on Abraham's bosom (chest)! (See John 13:23 as an example.)

By using that example, Jesus Christ the LORD was conveying to the Jews that it was futile to believe in Abraham in order to be saved. That point was further revealed by the comments, which the rich man made to Abraham and by Abraham's response. The rich man said, "[24] Father Abraham, have mercy on me, and send Lazarus, that he may dip the tip of his finger in water, and cool my tongue; for I am tormented in this flame." (After Judah rejected Christ the LORD of host, Judah lost the Promised Land, has been persecuted, hated, ridiculed, tormented, and rejected throughout the world. See Deuteronomy chapter 28; 1 Kings 9:3-9.)

But Abraham replied and said, "[25] Son, remember

that thou [you] in thy [your] lifetime receivedst thy good things [the blessing of God], and likewise Lazarus evil things: but now he is comforted, and thou art tormented. 26 And beside all this, between us and you there is a great gulf fixed: so that they which would pass from hence to you cannot; neither can they pass to us, that would come from thence." In other words, salvation cannot be obtained from you (Judah) any more; the Gospel is given to the Gentiles. Therefore, "there is a great gulf fixed" "between us," that is, between Judah and Abraham, and between Judah and Lazarus (the Gentiles).

And, as if Abraham had this hierarchy of authority above God, the rich man (Judah) said to Abraham, "27 I pray thee therefore, father, that thou wouldest send him to my father's house: 28 For I have five brethren; that he may testify unto them, lest they also come into this place of torment." Luke 16:27, 28

The "five" brothers that the rich man (Judah) is referring to are the brothers, which Leah conceived while she and Jacob lived in an area called Haran (northwestern part of Iraq), which was during the time Jacob was in servitude to Laban, his father-in-law, for fourteen years. The record confirms that Judah had five brothers. They are as follows: "22 Now the sons of Israel [Jacob] were twelve. 23 The sons of Leah: Reuben, Jacob's first born, and Simeon, and Levi, and Judah, and Issachar, and Zebulun" (Genesis 35:22, 23).

In passing, let me make one point regarding the five brothers (tribes) of Judah. Since Jesus is acknowledging that Lazarus can reach the five tribes, it confirms the fact that these five tribes are not lost, as many would like us to believe. (See 2 Chronicles 15:8-10.)

As you can readily see in the parable, Christ the LORD reveals that Judah had five brothers. And now, since the rich man (Judah) realizes that he is rejected by God, he is asking Abraham to send Lazarus, the Gentile, to warn his five brothers (five tribes) of their peril. But again, Abraham emphasizes and directs Judah to consult the writing of Moses for their salvation.

Once more, Christ drives the point home to His audience that faith in Abraham will not save Judah, his "father's house," or his "five brethren." The only way for his brothers to be saved is to believe in the God of Abraham, and that is Jesus Christ the LORD of hosts, as we know Him now in the New Testament.

The information regarding his brother's salvation is recorded in the Torah (the five books of Moses); and that salvation comes, as always, from Christ the LORD of hosts who lived in the "most holy place" of His Sanctuary in "Shiloh," and later, in Jerusalem, in the Sanctuary that was built by King Solomon.

Referring to his son Judah, Jacob (Israel) foretold of "Shiloh" coming to His people through the lineage of Judah. Jacob said, "[10] The sceptre shall not depart from Judah, nor a lawgiver from between his feet, until Shiloh come; and unto Him shall the gathering of the people be" (Genesis 49:10).

Unfortunately, as you can see in the parable of the rich man and Lazarus, the rich man (Judah) would not repent or allow "the gathering of the people" to take place

## Lazarus and the Rich Man

"unto Him [Shiloh]." (Shiloh refers to Christ the LORD of hosts. See 1 Samuel 4:4.) The Jews said that He (Shiloh) was a fraud, an imposture, a liar, a blasphemer, and the list goes on and on. And, at the end of His three and a half years of ministry, they mocked Him and rejected Him (John 1:11). Therefore, "The sceptre" did "depart from Judah," and the "lawgiver [Exodus 20:1, 2] from between his feet." And when Judah rejected the Gospel of Jesus Christ the LORD, which was preached to them, by Him and by the apostles, the apostles finally went and directed their preaching to the Gentiles (Acts 13:46-48). And when the Gentiles heard the Gospel message, they wholeheartedly accepted its message and Christ the LORD as their LORD God and Savior.

The Gentiles accepted Christ the LORD of hosts as their LORD God and Savior, as Abraham, Moses, and the rest of the prophets of the Old Testament had. Now, Christ the LORD was the God of the Gentiles because Judah rejected Him and did not want to carry on with His Gospel. Therefore, Christ the LORD of hosts foretold of this event when He said by the pen of Hosea, "[23] I will say to them which were not My people, Thou [you] are My people; and they shall say, Thou [You] art my God" (Hosea 2:23).

Therefore to accentuate Judah's rejection of Christ (Shiloh) and His salvation, Jesus portrays Abraham's counsel as follows: "[29] Abraham saith unto him [the rich man], They have Moses and the prophets; let them hear them" (Luke 16:29).

Did they?

In this parable, Abraham is said to be giving wise counsel to the Jews. They were to go to Moses' writings in order to verify Christ's authenticity, Christ's claims, and of the coming events that would effect the Jews and Gentiles. But, if they took the time to read what Moses has written about the LORD God of their fathers, they would have found out that he truly wrote about Christ the LORD of hosts and that Christ is really the LORD God of their fathers.

But Judah, during Christ's time, refused to go and search the Scriptures in order to verify Christ's claims that He is the LORD God of their fathers. They thought that He cannot be the Mighty God of our fathers because He is a mere man! But, if Jesus came in His spirit form with all of His power and might, as He did on top of Mount Sinai, how was He going to be sacrificed by the hands of men?

Would they somehow be able to reach out heavenward and capture Him?

Needless to say, obviously not!

Therefore, Christ the God of Abraham came in the flesh as He had promised and offered Himself a sacrifice for the penitent sinners; but knowing that the Jews would reject Him and refused to accept His atoning sacrifice for their sins, Jesus said to them, "45 Do not think that I will accuse you to the Father: there is one that accuseth you, even Moses, in whom ye [all of you] trust. 46 For had ye believed Moses, ye would have believed Me: for he wrote of Me. 47 But if ye believe not his writings how shall ye believe my words?" John 5:45-47

But the Jewish callous heart did not want to hear what Moses and Christ had to say. They were more interested in a "sign" (Luke 11:16). But, a sign was not going to be given to them, except for the "sign" of Jonah. They had the Scriptures, why did they need a "sign"?

Knowing that fact, Christ revealed their rejection of Him, by the following words: "30 And he [the rich man] said, Nay, father Abraham; but if one went unto them from the dead, they will repent." Luke 16:30

Did they repent when they listened to those individuals that were resurrected by Christ? Did they listen to Lazarus, who was resurrected by Christ couple of weeks after this incident? Many did; but the majority of the Jewish leaders were offended by Christ and sought to kill Him.

In conclusion, Jesus added, "31 If they hear not Moses and the prophets, neither will they be persuaded, though one rose from the dead." Luke 16:31

Needless to say, Jesus was right; many of the Jews were not persuaded by the many individuals that were resurrected during Christ three and a half years of ministry and by Moses' testimony. And at the end, they did not want to believe that the Messiah, "which is being interpreted the Christ" (John 1:41), had also risen from the dead. And because of those disbeliefs, as the parable indicates, Lazarus found himself favored by Abraham and the rich man was rejected by Abraham, in whom he trusted because Abraham had no power to save him.

## Saul and the Witch at Endor

Is Samuel the prophet of the LORD really alive as a spirit being?

The record states: "7 Then said Saul unto his servants, Seek me a woman that hath a familiar spirit, that I may go to her, and enquire of her. And his servants said to him, Behold, there is a woman that hath a familiar spirit at Endor. 8 And Saul disguised himself, and put on other raiment, and he went, and two men with him, and they came to the women by night: and he said, I pray thee, divine unto me by the familiar spirit, and bring me him up, whom I shall name unto thee. 9 And the woman said unto him, Behold, thou knowest what Saul hath done, how he hath cut off those that have familiar spirits, and the wizards, out of the land: wherefore then layest thou a snare for my life, to cause me to die? 10 And Saul sware to her by the LORD, saying, As the LORD liveth, there shall no punishment happen to thee for this thing. 11 Then said the woman, Whom shall I bring up unto thee? And he said, Bring me up Samuel. 12 And when the woman saw Samuel, she cried with a loud voice; and the woman spake to Saul, saying, Why hast thou deceived me? for thou art Saul. 13 And the king said unto her, Be not afraid: for what sawest thou? And the woman said unto Saul, I saw gods ascending out of the earth. 14 And he said unto her, What form is he of? And she said, An old man cometh up; and he is covered with a mantle. And Saul perceived that it was Samuel, and he stooped with his face to the ground, and bowed himself.

"15 And Samuel said to Saul, Why hast thou disquieted me, to bring me up? And Saul answered, I am sore distressed, for the Philistines make war against me, and God is departed from me, and answereth me no more, neither by prophets, nor by dreams: therefore I have called thee, that thou mayest made known unto me what I shall do. 16 Then said Samuel, Wherefore then dost thou ask of me, seeing the LORD is departed from thee, and is become thine enemy? 17 And the LORD hath done to him, as he spake by me:

for the LORD hath rent the kingdom out of thine hand, and given it to thy neighbour, even to David: 18 Because thou obeyedst not the voice of the LORD, nor executedst His fierce wrath upon Amalek, therefore hath the LORD done this thing unto thee this day. 19 Moreover the LORD will also deliver Israel with thee into the hand of the Philistines; and to morrow shalt thou and thy sons be with me: the LORD also shall deliver the host of Israel into the hand of the Philistines." 1 Samuel 28:7-19

Although we have studied earlier about individuals who were devil possessed, let us look at the events briefly, before the creation of the earth took place by Christ the LORD of hosts, in order to understand the above verses and who it is the witch of Endor divined for King Saul.

Recently, the scientific community has gone on a limb and stated that the universe is about twelve and a half billion years old.

But, regarding planet earth, they have stated that the earth is about four and a half billion years old.

If that is their finding, it can be said that their finding coincides with Genesis 1:2 where Moses says, "2 And the earth was without form, and void; and darkness was upon the face of the deep" (Genesis 1:2).

In addition, regarding the ecosystem of the earth, the scientific community has also stated that it came into existence less than three billion years ago.

Since that is their finding, it places the beginning of the creation week, of Genesis 1:3-31, to be less than three billion years old; furthermore, it also makes our moon and sun less than three billion years old because they were created on the fourth day of the creation week. (See

Genesis 1:14-19.)

Therefore, we can conclude; since sin entered, about six thousand years ago, on planet earth, by the deceptive temptation of Satan, it means that sin had to come into fruition sometime after the creation week because prior and during the creation week of Genesis 1:1-31, sin had not entered in the entire universe or in the third heaven. Prior to the creation week, there was no discord amongst the created beings of the universe or in the third heaven. We are told, "7 When the morning stars [angels] sang together, and all the sons [the rest of the created beings in the universe] of God shouted for joy?" Job 38:7

That being a Scriptural fact, it means that Satan's evil work had to start sometime after the creation week and during the three billion years of tranquility and bliss, which existed before sin entered planet earth.

And so it was, sin did enter in the third heaven by the deceptive work of Satan two billion years after the creation week; and sin entered on earth through Eve and Adam one billion years after Satan sinned. And after sin entered on earth, the prophet of the LORD states that "7 there was war in heaven: Michael and His angels fought against the dragon [Satan, Rev. 12:9]: and the dragon fought and his angels" (Revelation 12:7).

Therefore, before sin entered on planet earth, six thousand years ago, sin already had entered in the third heaven. And since Satan and his evil angels did not want to repent and be saved from their eternal demise (See Jude 6.), they were kicked out of their heavenly abode, and landed upon planet earth.

In reference to that event, Christ the LORD of hosts "18 said unto them [the 70; Luke 10:17], I beheld Satan as lightning fall from heaven" (Luke 10:18).

And in reference to that heavenly war, the prophet of the LORD says, "12 Therefore rejoice, ye heavens, and ye that dwell in them," because Satan and his evil angels have been kicked out of heaven; but he warns the inhabitants of the earth by saying, "Woe to the inhabiters of the earth and of the sea! for the devil [Satan] is come down unto you, having great wrath, because he knoweth that he hath but a short time" (Revelation 12:12).

According to the above verses, Satan and his evil angels have been kicked out of heaven and landed upon planet earth to live with the human beings because Satan and his evil angels had nowhere else to go. They were forced to live with the human race because Adam and Eve, out of the whole universe, rebelled against Christ the LORD of hosts and threw their allegiance with Satan. In doing so, they forfeited the dominion of planet earth (Genesis 1:28), to Satan, which was given to them by Christ the LORD of hosts.

And ever since that time, Satan and his evil angels have been destroying men, women, and children through pride, diseases, wars, famine, hate, crimes, drugs, alcohol, prostitution, cigarettes, lies, money, deceptions, etc., etc. That is why the prophet of the LORD warns the inhabitants of the earth by saying, "8 Be sober, be vigilant; because your adversary the devil, as a roaring lion, walketh about, seeking whom he may devour" (1 Peter 5:8).

## Saul and the Witch of Endor

For more detailed information on the above subject, read my book called, "According to a Promise" *By: Philip Mitanidis.* BEEHIVE PUBLISHING HOUSE INC.

Satan and his evil angels, today, as before, are seeking to devour whom they can by any means and that includes their favorite tool—deception.

Therefore, the story of King Saul and the witch of Endor is a classic story of satanic deception, better known today in the realm of ghosts, ghouls, spirits, paranormal, psychics, mystics, diviners, seers, mediums, apparitions, etc., etc.

So! What is a witch, a seer, or a medium?

A simple explanation, according to the Bible prophets, a medium, a witch, or a seer is an individual who is possessed by a "familiar spirit (s)." And that "familiar spirit (s)" provides the medium, seer, or witch with information that was requested by the customer or in this case by King Saul.

Furthermore, in order to remove any assumptions and confusion, regarding the meaning of what is or are "familiar spirit [s]," let the inspired Scriptures (Bible) explain what or who is or are "familiar spirit [s]."

As per the Bible, a "familiar spirit" is a spirit or spirits that occupy or reside in an unrepentant person's body. Familiar spirits are identified, throughout the Scriptures, as "[14] the spirits of devils [Satan's evil angels], working miracles, which go forth unto the kings of the earth and of the whole world, to gather them to the battle of that great day of God Almighty" (Revelation 16:14).

In essence then, a "familiar spirit" or "spirits" are

## Saul and the Witch of Endor

identified as the heavenly angels who rebelled in heaven, were kicked out of heaven, and landed on earth to live (Rev. 12:7-9). Now, these satanic evil angels are "working miracles" through those un-repented individuals whom they possess. (An "unrepentant individual" is an individual who "loves unrighteousness" and "hates truth." 2 Thessalonians 2:12.)

In reference to unrepentant sinners and possessed individuals, by satanic evil spirits (familiar spirits), here is an example taken from the book of Acts chapter nineteen.

It reads as follows:

> "[13] certain of the vagabond Jews, exorcists, took upon them to call over them which had evil spirits the name of the LORD Jesus, saying, We adjure you by Jesus whom Paul preacheth. [14] And there were seven sons of one Sceva, a Jew, and chief of the priests, which did so. [15] And the evil spirit answered and said, Jesus I know, and Paul I know; but who are ye [all of you]? [16] And the man in whom the evil spirit was leaped on them, and overcame them, and prevailed against them, so that they fled out of that house naked and wounded. [17] And this was known to all the Jews and Greeks also dwelling at Ephesus; and fear fell on them all, and the name of the LORD Jesus was magnified" (Acts 19:13-17).

After that story got around, many of the people who were involved in sorcery and witchcraft "[19] brought their books together, and burned them before all men: and counted the price of them, and found it fifty thousand pieces of silver." And then the prophet of the LORD adds, "[20] So mighty grew the word of God and prevailed" over their sorcery and magic. Acts 19:19, 20.

As you have read in the above verses, the familiar spirits (devils) chased (v.16) those who tried to make them leave the bodies of the individuals, whom they possessed.

In fact, about one thousand and five hundred and thirty years, before the above event took place, when the children of Israel moved into the Promised Land (Canaan), they were admonished not to tolerate anyone that had a "familiar spirit." All of the Promised Land was to be cleared from people who practiced witchcraft because Christ the LORD of hosts lived there, in His Sanctuary, which was pitched in a place called "Shiloh." That is why the witch at Endor became defensive towards her customers. She knew that she was not to practice witchcraft; and even if she was tricked to divine, she would have been killed. Therefore, she quickly said to King Saul, "9 Behold, thou [you] knowest what Saul hath done, how he hath cut off those that have familiar spirits, and the wizards, out of the land: wherefore then layest thou a snare for my life, to cause me to die?" 1 Samuel 28:9. But King Saul replied, "Be not afraid," and then he asked her what did she see (v.13)? And the witch "13 said unto Saul, I saw gods ascending out of the earth. 14 And he said unto her, What form is he of? And she said, An old man cometh up; and he is covered with a mantle. And Saul perceived that it was Samuel, and he stooped with his face to the ground, and bowed himself" (1 Samuel 28:13, 14).

Even though there is no proof presented or stated, in the above verses that an actual immortal man or an immortal spirit or an immortal soul of Samuel was presented to King Saul, by the witch of Endor, the immortal soul believers still insist that it was Samuel who came up out of the earth to talk to King Saul!

But contrary to that belief, Scripturally because Samuel, like the rest of us, was a sinner, he died (Romans 6:23). And when he died, Samuel, like the rest of the dead, has no recollection of God; or as the psalmist puts it; "4 His breath goeth forth, he returneth to his earth; in that very day his thoughts perish" (Psalms 146:4). And in reference to God, the psalmist says, "5 in death there is no remembrance of Thee [You]" (Psalms 6:5). And again we are told that "17 The dead praise not the LORD" (Psalms 115:17).

So! Since Samuel has no recollection of God or anyone else because his thoughts have perished, how can he be interacting with the witch of Endor?

And, to further dispute the claim that Samuel's spirits or souls or body is alive in heaven, Christ the LORD of hosts has stated that no man has gone to heaven (John 3:13). That being a fact, how can Samuel be alive and gone to heaven, as the immortal soul believers claim? In fact, in none of the above verses you will find that Samuel's immortal soul or spirit came from heaven to visit King Saul? In stead, what you do find in the above verses is the witch's familiar evil spirit (evil angel) impersonating Samuel. In fact, Satan and his evil angels can transform themselves into what ever they want. They can pose as trees, dogs, people, cats, etc. They have that ability.

We are told:

## Saul and the Witch of Endor

> "14 Satan himself is transformed into an angel of light. 15 Therefore it is no great thing if his ministers also be transformed as the ministers of righteousness; whose end shall be according to their works" (2 Corinthians 11:14, 15).

Having said that, now further observe what happened in the cave of the witch of Endor, which is south-west from the southern tip of the Sea of Galilee. King Saul went to a witch to seek guidance regarding the war with the Philistines. The reason he went to see the witch was due to the fact that God would not interact (v.15) with King Saul anymore because of Saul's sins. In his desperation, King Saul, knowing better not to go to individuals who were devil possessed (those who have familiar spirits in them), did go to see a witch who had a familiar spirit (19). And when King Saul asked the woman what did she see; she said that she saw "gods ascending out of the earth [v.13]." Then, King Saul, as if he could not see the distorted figures forming and coming out of the ground, asked her again, "What form is he of? And she said, An old man cometh up; and he is covered with a mantle. And Saul perceived that it was Samuel, and he stooped with his face to the ground, and bowed himself" (v.14).

Although King Saul was present during the events that were taking place before his eyes because of the distorted figures, he like the witch could not perceive what they were looking at? In fact, King Saul even asked the witch "What form is he of?" (v.14) Therefore, they both assumed it was Samuel who came up out of the earth because that is for whom King Saul asked the witch

to divine for. The record states, "Saul perceived" that the "old man," who was covered with a mantle, "was Samuel" (v.14). In other words, the witch did not actually see Samuel; she assumed that it was Samuel and informed Saul of that assumption. And, in turn, Saul accepted that assumption and "bowed himself" towards the "ground."

Since that is what the record states, verse fourteen creates some very severe contradictions for the immortal soul or spirit believers.

If Samuel was in heaven, in a spirit form, why was he "coming out of the earth"?

And, if Samuel was present in the cave of Endor, why would his presence be distorted?

If Samuel went to heaven, he would have put on a youthful immortality and would not come up "out of the earth" unrecognizable as an "old man" "covered with a mantle."

And we can further ask, "What is Samuel doing in the earth, wearing old clothes instead of the robe of righteousness, if he is one of the righteous men who is gone into heaven to be with Christ the LORD of hosts?"

But, on a more serious note, since the immortal soul theorists believe that the righteous go to heaven to be with the LORD, how is it that Samuel took upon Himself to come down from heaven to talk with King Saul when God Himself refused to talk to Saul (v.15)?

Does that mean that Samuel bypassed Christ's authority and Christ's decision, which was not to talk to King Saul? By bypassing Christ's authority, why did Samuel take upon himself to come down to the earth, via

## Saul and the Witch of Endor

the witch, to inform Saul that he and his sons were going to be killed by the Philistines the next day and be with him and not with Christ the LORD of hosts?

By the way, did you notice? Samuel was doing the very same thing King Saul was not suppose to do; and that is, make contact with the witch—any witch? Should not these two men respected God's decision, and refrained from interacting with the witch and with the "familiar spirits"?

But, on a more gruesome note—if we think like the immortal soul believers—since it was the witch of Endor who summoned Samuel to come up out of the earth, via her "familiar spirit" (satanic evil angel), that indicates that Samuel is living in the realm of the satanic abode—in the earth somewhere and not in heaven. In fact, heaven is not mentioned in 1 Samuel 28:7-19. Therefore the immortal soul believers cannot say that Samuel is in heaven because according to 1 Samuel 28:7-19, Samuel is controlled or influenced by Satan, his satanic evil angels, and by the witch of Endor; and that scenario places Samuel under Satan's domain and under Satan's authority.

Under those conditions, do the immortal soul believers still want to believe in the immortal soul doctrine?

Furthermore, since only God knows the future, how did Samuel know that Saul and his two sons were going to be killed the next day, by avoiding Christ's authority? He did not know; it was the familiar spirit's intent to verbally wound and demoralize Saul with a vindictive remark in order to cause Saul to abandon God.

In addition, if Samuel was alive in heaven and knew what was happening to King Saul, why did he not appear to King Saul without the help of the witch? Did Samuel need a satanic evil angel to summon him? Does Satan or any of his evil angels have the authority over all of those who live in heaven; and therefore they can summon anyone at will from heaven?

Really!

Where is the Scripture to substantiate that fact?

Please stop and think for a moment; how can these outcasts (Satan and his satanic angels) have that kind of an authority and power when they are not allowed to travel anywhere in the universe, let alone go to the third heaven and summon someone to do their bidding?

By the way, even if Samuel was in heaven, it would not be possible for him to know what King Saul was up to, or anyone else on planet earth. Samuel would be oblivious to what is taking place on earth, just as we are oblivious to what is going on in heaven. Heaven is billions upon billions of light years away from earth, how would Samuel be able to see or know what was happening down here? He does not have those kinds of capabilities; only God has those abilities.

Furthermore Samuel does not have any authority to come to planet earth on his own volition and interfere with the plan of salvation for a perishing world?

But, if Samuel was in heaven because of his love for Christ the LORD, he would not bypass Christ's decisions; if he did he would sin. If that is what he did, via the witch, it means that Christ's authority and decision

## Saul and the Witch of Endor

was not good enough for Samuel to abide by? Therefore, Samuel disobeyed Christ the LORD and came to planet earth at the witch's command?

If Samuel was in heaven, why did he choose to disobey Christ the LORD, when all along, while he was alive on earth, Samuel refused to talk to King Saul after King Saul rebelled and disobeyed Christ's command?

How is it possible for Samuel to make all of those rebellious decisions without the consent of Christ the LORD of hosts?

Is Samuel above Christ the LORD of hosts; is that why he took matters in his own hands and came to talk with King Saul?

Who is in charge in heaven, Christ or Samuel?

There is something wrong with the belief that Samuel's spirit or soul is immortal, alive, and gone to heaven; and somewhere along the way, Samuel became rebellious by taking upon himself to over-ride Christ's decision and came to planet earth to communicate with Saul through, of all people, the witch of Endor?

If that is what happened, as the argument for the immortal soul implies, then we can say that there is a sinner in heaven by the name of Samuel.

Now what?

Although we can continue to argue the events of the witch of Endor, King Saul, and Samuel, I prefer Scripture to settle any arguments relating to the witch, Saul, and Samuel. And Scripture plainly states that "⁵ the living know that they shall die; but the dead know not any thing" (Ecclesiastes 9:5).

## Saul and the Witch of Endor

Therefore, we can say that there is something wrong with the belief that a witch, Satan, or his satanic evil angels have any form of authority to summon anyone from the universe, contrary to the will of Christ the LORD of hosts, to come to earth, in order to deceive the human race into eternal perdition.

Obviously there is something wrong with that belief because we are told that none of the righteous created beings, who live throughout the universe and in the third heaven, take it upon themselves to override Christ's commands. If they did, they would be rebellious and outcasts and full of sin like Satan and his evil angels. And if they become rebellious, at any point of time, they would be full of sin. And when that happens, they would not be able to live or be with Christ the LORD of hosts. Like Samuel, they would eventually decay and die (Romans 6:23) because they do not have or possess immortality. We are told only God has immortality (1 Timothy 6:16).

Because of that Biblical fact, Samuel was not the one in the cave who appeared before King Saul; it was the witch's evil satanic angel called "familiar spirit" who impersonated the prophet Samuel.

Please remember; if Samuel possessed immortality, or any part of him, he could not be killed, hurt, tortured, burnt by fire, or destroyed. Therefore an immortal soul would be impervious to hell. But because man is "mortal" (Job 4:17), all of the above can be imposed upon him; and at the end, he would become ashes or dust, if he is not saved by Christ's grace.

Therefore because Samuel is "mortal," he, like King David, is dead and buried in his grave (Acts 2:29). And, like King David, Samuel has "not ascended into heaven" (Acts 2:34) because, like King David, Samuel does not possess immortality; only God possesses immortality.

And because of that Biblical fact, Samuel and King David are still in their graves waiting for the resurrection of the righteous to take place (John 5:28, 29). They are waiting to be resurrected by Christ the LORD of hosts; and, at that time, they will be given immortality because both Samuel and King David, like the rest of us, do not have or possess immortality.

Let me say again with the prophet of the LORD, only God has immortality.

Here is the acknowledgement regarding that fact:

> "$_{15}$ Which in his times he shall shew, who is the blessed and only Potentate, the King of kings, and Lord of lords; $_{16}$ Who only hath immortality, dwelling in the light which no man can approach unto; whom no man hath seen, nor can see: to whom be honour and power everlasting. Amen." 1 Timothy 6:15, 16 (See 1 Timothy 1:17 also.)

That being a Biblical fact, why do people who believe in the Bible still believe in disembodied immortal souls or spirits?

Should they, according to Scripture, believe the

prophet's words when he says, only God has immortality?
Should they?
What do you think?

~ ~ ~

"19 And when they shall say unto you, Seek unto them that have familiar spirits, and unto wizards that peep, and that mutter: should not a people seek unto their God? for the living to the dead" (Isaiah 8:19).

## What is the Spirit of Man

Needless to say, according to the Bible, death is opposite to life. So! Why do people say that man lives on? They do because they have been taught, perhaps from their youth, to believe, for whatever reason that man has an eternal spirit, which lives within him.

Although there is no such Biblical doctrine to support that belief, people insist that there is an entity called spirit, which occupies the body of a person, and at death, they claim, the spirit of that person continues to live on somewhere in heaven or hell?

As I have stated before, this doctrinal belief cannot be found in the inspired Scriptures (Bible).

To clear the confusion of what is the spirit of man, try a little experiment; ask several people what is the spirit of man, and then, ask them to identify the spirit of man. In their response, notice if the spirit of man is the thinking part of man's brain; or is the thinking part of man's brain a separate entity from the brain? And, if the spirit of man is a separate entity, which dwells within a person and thinks for itself and for the person it occupies, does that mean, a person's thinking part (the brain) has no say in what a person thinks or does?

If we accept the belief that it is this separate entity, called "spirit," which thinks for itself and for man, do you think that this separate entity, called "spirit," should be held accountable for all of the physical and verbal actions it causes a person to do? If you accept that it is this separate spirit entity, which causes a person to react to its wishes, should that spirit be held accountable for the sins it has committed and not the person it occupies?

Personally, and as per Scripture, the spirit, should be held accountable and die because of the sins it has committed (Romans 6:23). And, as far as the person it occupies is concerned that person should continue to live on because he or she has not willfully committed any sin.

What do you think, is that fair?

So, according to the above popular beliefs of immortal spirits, if a person's own brain does not think and cause the body to act verbally and physically, in a sinful manner, why does man die?

As per Scripture (Bible), man does die because by his own thoughts that are produced by his own brain, he has premeditated to sin and not some separate entity, called the spirit that lives within him.

As you can see, there is something wrong with the popular thinking of a separate immortal entity (spirit) living within a person. Scripture does not support a separate spirit, which occupies the body, thinks for the body, or for the brain. As we have studied before, the verse or verses do not exist in the entire Bible. But what does exist is the fact that there are a number of references to the use of the word spirit that are mentioned in the Bible. You can review the word spirit, in the appendix, under the heading of *"The Use of the Words Soul and Spirit."*

For now, here are few examples. Biblically, there is the spirit of God the Father, the spirit of God the Christ, and the spirit of God the Holy Spirit. And there is the spirit of man (2 Corinthians 2:13), "the spirit of the world" (1 Corinthians 2:12), "the spirit of meekness" (1

Corinthians 4:21), the "spirit of faith" (2 Corinthians 4:13), and so on.

In addition, the word spirit sometimes is referred to as "wind" (Exodus 10:13; Jonah 1:4; Genesis 6:17), "tempest" (Psalms 11:6), "smell" (Leviticus 26:31; Genesis 8:21), "breath" (Genesis 6:17), "mind" (Genesis 26:35), etc., etc., but never as immortal.

As you have noticed, the above references, and like references, do not support an immortal separate spirit, which occupies the body, thinks for the body, or for the brain. There is no Scripture to suggest otherwise.

So! What is the spirit of man?

According to the Bible, the spirit of man is referred to as the thinking part of the man's physical brain, which consists of the firing of electronic currents across the synopsis and through the billions of dendrites in search of stored information in the brain. Without the electronic current crossing the synopsis in the brain, man cannot think or function verbally and physically.

Therefore, the thinking part of the brain that is activated by the roaming electronic currents in the brain, which search for stored information in the brain, is the spirit of man.

Here are the Biblical references, which reveal what is man's spirit.

"[10] But God has revealed them unto us by his Spirit: for the Spirit searcheth all things, yea, the deep things of God. [11] For what man knoweth the things of a man, save the spirit of man which is in him? even so the things of God knoweth no man, but the Spirit of God" (1

Corinthians 2:10, 11).

Thus, according to the above verses, the "Spirit of God" is the thinking part of God, which searches "the deep things of God" (1 Corinthians 2:10). Jesus Christ the LORD of hosts said, "Surely as I have thought, so shall it come to pass; and as I have purposed, so shall it stand" (Isaiah 14:24).

Likewise, the thinking part of the brain is referred to as "the spirit of your mind" (Ephesians 4:23). Therefore, the inner function of the brain, which is the thinking part (spirit) of man, is revealed as the one that searches the inner stored information in the brain in order to know "the things of man" (1 Corinthians 2:11). And when man dies because of his sin, "4 His breath goeth forth, he returneth to his earth; in that very day his thoughts perish" (Psalms 146:4).

Therefore when man dies, his spirit (the thinking part of the brain) also dies (ceases to exist) because the brain, like the body, decays in the grave into dust.

But, as we have read before, there is another spirit that is in man; and that spirit is identified as the sustaining spirit or life force that is given, by Christ the LORD of hosts, to man, in order to sustain him.

Here are the references: "7 And the LORD God formed man of the dust of the ground, and breathed into his nostrils the breath of life; and man became a living soul" (Genesis 2:7).

Now we can ask; what does "the breath of life" consist?

We are told: "14 If He [God] set His heart upon

man, if He gather unto Himself His spirit and His breath; 15 All flesh shall perish together, and man shall turn again unto dust" (Job 34:14, 15).

So the "spirit" that is given to man is of God. It is God's life force (spirit) that sustains man. The life force, which sustains the universe and everything that is in it, is by the word of Christ the LORD of hosts. We are told, "4 In Him [Christ] was life; and the life was the light of men" (John 1:4). "17 and by Him [Christ] all things consist" (Colossians 1:17). "7 the heavens and the earth, which are now, by the same word are kept in store" (2 Peter 3:7).

Therefore the "spirit" that sustains the universe and everything that is in it is of Christ the LORD of hosts. And when man dies, "7 the spirit shall return unto God [Christ the LORD of hosts] who gave it" (Ecclesiastes 12:7).

Notably, according to the above references, man possesses two characteristics. First, we noted that man has a capacity to think with his brain; and that thinking process is referred to in the Bible as "spirit."

Secondly, we are told that man has another "spirit" that is given to him by Christ the LORD of hosts in order to keep man alive; and that "spirit," which sustains man, goes back to God who gave it, when man dies.

Therefore according to the above verses, however you want to think—no pun intended—of the spirit of man, there is nothing in the word "spirit," the thinking part of man's physical brain, to suggest that it is a separate entity in the makeup of man, which thinks for man and possesses eternal life; and therefore it goes to heaven or hell when man dies.

In support of what I have said above, let me leave you with one very predominant sobering Scripturall fact, which disperses the idea that man's spirit is immortal, and therefore, it lives on somewhere when man dies.

If you believe that the spirit of man possesses immortality, I have to ask, where did it acquire immortality? I ask that question because the Bible tells us only God has immortality (1 Timothy 6:13-16.); none of the created beings throughout the universe and in the third heaven possess immortality.

So! How is it possible for the sinful spirit of man to live on forever, when it does not possess immortality?

~ ~ ~

"48 What man is he that liveth, and shall not see death? shall he deliver his soul from the hand of the grave?" "32 Yet shall he be brought to the grave, and shall remain in the tomb." Psalms 89:48; Job 21:32.

# APPENDIX

## *THE USE OF THE WORDS SOUL & SPIRIT*

1). In the Old Testament, the Hebrew word "nephesh" (נפש) occurs over 740 times; it is translated to read "soul" over 470 times. And the rest of the time, it is translated over 40 times to read life, breath, wind, ghosts, and so on.

In the New Testaments, the Greek word "psuhe" (ψυχη) occurs 100 times; it is translated to read "soul" over 55 times; the rest of the times it is translated to read "breath," "wind," and so on.

2). The word "spirit" is translated over 440 times from the Hebrew word "ruah." It is translated to read "spirit" over 230 times.

The Greek word "pneuma" (πνευμα) in the New Testament is mentioned on the overall about 380 times. It is translated to read "spirit" about 290 times and about 90 times "wind."

3). The word "hell," in the Old Testament is derived from the Hebrew words "sheol" and "nephesh."

In the New Testament, the word "hell" is derived from the Greek words "tartaros," "hades," and "gehenna."

The words "soul" and "spirit," in the Bible, are never said to possess immortality. They can be killed and die.

# QUETIONS

1. Who created Adam and Eve?

2. How were Adam and Eve Created?

3. Were Adam and Eve created mortal?

4. Who said to Adam and Eve if they sinned they would die?

5. Who said to Adam and Eve if they sinned they would not die.

6. Does man have an immortal soul?

7. A soul that sins, does it die?

8. What does a soul turn into when it dies?

9. Is there such a place as hell?

10. Is anybody in hell today?

11. How many resurrections of the dead are there?

12. Who will resurrect the dead and when?

13. What is the end result of the righteous dead and living, and of the unrighteous dead and living?

14. Where are the dead right now? *(Answer.)* *See Revelation 20:13, 14.*

15. Who only has immortality?

BIBLIOGRAPHY

Mitanidis Philip.   *Christians Headed Into the Time of Trouble.*
BEEHIVE PUBLISHING HOUSE INC. Canada. 2007

Made in the USA